I0004075

Build a Help!

Build a HTML5 and CSS3 Website From Scratch

2025
Raphael Heide

Build a Help! Build a HTML5 and CSS3 Website From Scratch
Published by raphaelheide.com
Copyright ® 2025
No part of this publication may be reproduced, distributed, or transmitted in any form or by any means, including photocopying, recording, or other electronic or mechanical methods, without the prior written permission of the publisher, except as permitted by U.S. copyright law. For permission requests, contact https://raphaelheide.com

LIMIT OF LIABILITY / DISCLAIMER OF WARRANTY: The publisher and the author make no representations or warranties with respect to the accuracy or completeness of the contents of this work and specifically disclaim all warranties, including without limitation warranties of fitness for a particular purpose. No warranty may be created or extended by sales or promotional materials. The advice and strategies contained herein may not be suitable for every situation. This work is sold with the understanding that the publisher and the author are not engaged in rendering financial, regulatory, investment, or other professional services.

Heide, Raphael 2025 Help! Build a HTML5 and CSS3 Website From Scratch

The "Help!" series is your comprehensive guide to navigating the intricacies of the online world with ease and confidence. In this series of books, we dive into the step-by-step processes of various online activities, from setting up subscriptions to canceling accounts and everything in between. Whether you are a tech-savvy individual or just starting your online journey, these books are designed to demystify the digital landscape and empower you to manage your online interactions effortlessly.

THANK YOU TO MY READERS

I want to express my sincere gratitude for choosing our "Help!" series as your learning tool for mastering various online skills and actions. Your decision to invest in our comprehensive and up-to-date guide is truly appreciated, and my aim is to empower you to perform online tasks confidently and effortlessly.

I understand that navigating the digital landscape can be daunting, especially for beginners, but I have carefully crafted the content to make it accessible to users of all experience levels. My passion for helping others succeed in their online endeavors drives me to provide you with the best knowledge and techniques to accomplish your tasks effectively.

I hope that the knowledge you've gained from our series has proven valuable in your pursuit of mastering online activities. Your dedication to learning and growth is commendable, and I am honored to be a part of your journey.

I also want to extend my heartfelt thanks to those who have reached out with questions, feedback, and suggestions. Your engagement and interaction are invaluable to me. I am constantly seeking ways to improve and enhance our content, and your input helps me deliver a more enriching experience to all our readers.

In the spirit of community and collaboration, I invite you to stay connected with me. Whether you have further questions, need additional guidance, or wish to share your success stories, please don't hesitate to reach out. Your continued support is highly valued, and I am dedicated to assisting you in your online endeavors.

Once again, thank you for being a part of our readership. Your enthusiasm and dedication inspire me to continue creating valuable content and empowering individuals like you to achieve their online goals. I wish you ongoing success and fulfillment in all your future endeavors.

Warm regards,

Raphael Heide

SUMMARY

Introduction

Welcome to *Build an HTML5 and CSS3 Website From Scratch*! I'm Raphael Heide, and I'm thrilled to be your guide on this journey into the world of web design. Whether you're a complete beginner dreaming of your first website or someone looking to sharpen your skills, this book is for you. My goal is simple: to help you create a modern, functional, and great-looking website using two of the web's foundational tools—HTML5 and CSS—without needing any prior experience or fancy software.

In these pages, we'll start from the ground up. You'll learn how to structure a webpage with HTML5, the latest version of the language that powers the internet's content, and then bring it to life with CSS, the styling magic that controls colors, layouts, and more. This isn't just a theory book—you'll roll up your sleeves and build real projects alongside me. From crafting a simple homepage to designing a fully styled site, each chapter builds your skills step by step.

Why HTML5 and CSS3? They're the perfect starting point for anyone new to coding. HTML5 gives you the tools to create accessible, search-friendly webpages with features like video and interactive forms, while CSS3 lets you unleash your creativity with sleek designs that work on any device— phones, tablets, or desktops. Together, they're the backbone of every website you've ever visited, and by the end of this book, they'll be your tools too.

Here's how it works: we'll begin with the basics—how to write and save HTML files (always with a .html extension, as you'll see) and how to add CSS either within <style> tags or in separate .css files. I'll explain every step, with examples you can try yourself using just a text editor and a browser. No expensive tools, no complicated setups—just you, some code, and a bit of curiosity. As we go, you'll tackle practical projects, like building a blog or a small online store, and learn tricks to make your sites both functional and professional.

This book is hands-on and beginner-friendly, but it's not a race. Take your time, experiment with the code, and don't be afraid to mess up—some of my best lessons came from fixing my own mistakes. Each chapter includes clear instructions, snippets to test, and tips to keep you moving forward.

By the end, you won't just understand HTML5 and CSS3—you'll have a website you can proudly call your own.

So, grab a coffee (or tea, if that's your thing), open your text editor, and let's get started. The web is a blank canvas, and with this book, you're about to paint something amazing. Turn the page, and let's build something from scratch—together.

Raphael Heide

How to Read This Book?

Welcome to the exciting world of web design! Whether you're here to build your first website, tweak an existing project, or simply understand how the digital magic happens, this book is your guide. Think of it as a friendly companion—one that's here to walk you through the essentials, step by step, without drowning you in jargon. But before we dive into the nitty-gritty of code and creativity, let's set the stage. How should you approach this book? And what do you need to know to make the most of it? This chapter is all about getting you ready.

First things first: this book is hands-on. You won't just read about building websites—you'll *build* them. Each chapter introduces concepts like HTML (the structure of a webpage) and CSS (the style that makes it shine), and you'll put them into practice with examples and exercises. To follow along, you'll need a computer—any kind will do, whether it's a Mac, Windows, or Linux machine—and a simple text editor. Notepad (Windows), TextEdit (Mac), or something fancier like Visual Studio Code (which is free!) will work perfectly. No expensive software required. You'll also need a web browser, like Chrome or Firefox, to see your creations come to life.

Now, let's talk about the files you'll create. When we work with HTML—the language that defines a webpage's content, like headings and paragraphs—you'll save your work in files with a specific ending: .html. For example, if you write some HTML code to make a homepage, you'll save it as homepage.html. That .html extension tells your computer (and your browser) that this is a webpage file. It's like labeling a jar "cookies" so everyone knows what's inside. Throughout this book, whenever you see an instruction to create an HTML file, make sure to save it with that .html ending—otherwise, it won't work as expected.

Next up is CSS, the tool that adds color, layout, and flair to your HTML. CSS can live in two places, and we'll explore both in detail later. One option is inside your HTML file, tucked between <style> tags. These tags act like a little styling room within your webpage, where you can write rules like "make my text blue" or "center my heading." The other option is a separate file, saved with a .css extension—like styles.css. This external file is linked to your HTML, keeping your design rules organized and reusable across multiple pages. Don't worry if this sounds confusing now—later chapters will show you exactly how to set up both methods, with examples you can try yourself. For now, just know that CSS either goes inside <style> tags or in a .css file, and we'll unpack the "how" as we go.

So, how should you read this book? Start at the beginning and work your way through—each chapter builds on the last. If you're new to coding, take your time with the early sections on HTML and CSS basics. If you've dabbled before, feel free to skip to topics that catch your eye, like layouts or animations. Every chapter includes code snippets—short bits of HTML or CSS you can type out and test. I encourage you to do this! Open your text editor, create a new file, save it as test.html, and play with the examples. Seeing your code in action is the fastest way to learn.

You don't need to be a tech wizard to succeed here. This book assumes you're starting fresh, with curiosity as your only prerequisite. Mistakes are part of the process—your browser might show a blank page or a wonky design at first, and that's okay. We'll troubleshoot together. By the end, you'll have the skills to craft a website from scratch, whether it's a blog, a store, or something uniquely yours.

Ready? Turn the page, grab your text editor, and let's start building. The web is waiting for your ideas.

Chapter 1
What is a Website?

Picture this: you're standing in the middle of a bustling city square. To your left, there's a quirky little shop selling handmade trinkets. To your right, a towering billboard flashes the latest headlines. Ahead, a street performer strums a guitar, drawing a small crowd. Now imagine all of that—shops, signs, voices—shrunk down, digitized, and packed into a single glowing screen. That's a website: a slice of the internet where people, ideas, and creations come together, accessible to anyone, anywhere, with just a few clicks.

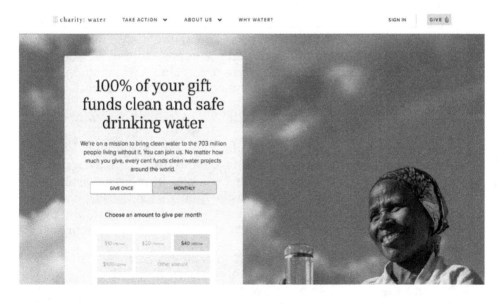

So, what exactly is a website? At its simplest, it's a collection of digital files—text, images, sounds, videos, and code—stored on a special computer called a server. This server isn't like the laptop on your desk; it's designed to stay awake 24/7, connected to the internet, waiting for someone to knock on its virtual door. When you type a web address (known as a URL, like www.raphaelheide.com) into your browser or click a link, you're sending a request to that server. It grabs the files, bundles them up, and sends them racing across the internet to your device, where they magically assemble into the page you see. It's a bit like ordering takeout—except instead of food, you get a perfectly arranged mix of words, pictures, and buttons.

But websites aren't just random piles of data. They're built with purpose. The backbone is usually HTML, which stands for HyperText Markup Language—a fancy way of saying it's the code that organizes everything into headings, paragraphs, and links. Then there's CSS (Cascading Style Sheets), the artist of the trio, which dresses up the page with colors, fonts, and layouts. And for the wow factor—think animations, pop-ups, or interactive quizzes—there's JavaScript, the code that makes things move and respond. Together, these tools turn a blank digital canvas into something useful, beautiful, or both. Don't worry if that sounds technical; you don't need to know how to write code to enjoy a website, just like you don't need to be a chef to savor a meal.

Websites come in all shapes and sizes, and they've evolved a lot since the internet's early days. Back in the 1990s, the first websites were simple— plain text, maybe a grainy photo or two, and a few clunky links. Think of them as digital pamphlets, mostly used by scientists and tech nerds to share notes. Today, though? Websites are entire worlds. There are static ones, like a "Contact Us" page for a small business that never changes. Then there are dynamic ones, like a news site that refreshes with breaking stories or a social media platform buzzing with posts and likes. Some websites are tiny—a single page with a poem or a recipe—while others, like Amazon or YouTube, are sprawling empires of code and content.

What makes websites special isn't just how they're built, but why. They're the internet's storytellers. A website can be a personal blog where someone pours out their thoughts, a virtual classroom teaching you to knit, or a marketplace where you can buy a vintage lamp from halfway across the globe. They're how businesses shout their brands, how artists display their portfolios, how governments share rules, and how friends argue about the best pizza toppings in a forum thread. Every website has a purpose, even if that purpose is just to make you laugh at a poorly animated dancing cat.

To really get it, let's break it down with an example. Say you visit www. thisisawebsite.com (not a real site, but go with it). The URL is like the address on a map—it tells your browser where to go. The "www" part is a tradition from the web's early days, signaling "world wide web," though plenty of sites skip it now. The "thisisawebsite" is the domain name, a human-friendly label for the server's actual address (a string of numbers called an IP address, like 192.168.1.1). And the ".com" at the end? That's the top-level domain, hinting at what the site's about—".com" for commercial, ".org" for organizations, ".edu" for schools, and so on. When you hit enter, your browser pings the server, the server dishes out the files, and suddenly you're reading about black holes or Martian sunsets.

Behind all this is a massive, invisible network called the internet—a web of cables, satellites, and signals tying the world together. Websites are the dots on that map, the places we visit when we explore it. And the crazy part? Anyone can make one. With a bit of know-how (or a user-friendly tool), you could launch your own site tomorrow—whether it's to sell cookies, rant about movies, or just say "hi" to the universe.

So why should you care about websites? Because they're how we live in the digital age. They're where we learn, shop, connect, and dream. They're the internet's beating heart, pulsing with information and possibility. And as you turn the pages of this book, we'll peel back more layers—how websites work, how they're made, and how they shape our world. For now, though, just know this: every time you open a browser, you're stepping into a limitless library, and every website is a story waiting to be tol

Chapter 2
How Browsers Render Websites

So, you've typed a URL into your browser say, www.raphaelheide.com and hit enter. A split second later, a shiny webpage pops up, complete with colorful buttons, crisp images, and snappy text. It feels instant, like flipping on a light switch. But behind that quick flash is a whirlwind of work your browser does to take a jumble of code and transform it into something you can scroll through. How does it pull that off? Let's peek under the hood and find out.

Your browser—whether it's Chrome, Firefox, Safari, or something else—is like a tireless translator, chef, and artist rolled into one. Its job is to fetch raw ingredients (files from a server) and whip them into a finished dish (the webpage). This process, called *rendering*, happens in a handful of steps, and while it's lightning-fast—usually under a second—it's a mini-marvel of modern tech. Here's how it goes down.

Step 1: The Request

It all starts when you tell the browser where to go. That URL you typed? It's the address of a server somewhere in the world. The browser kicks things off by sending a message across the internet: "Hey, server at www. raphaelheide.com, send me your stuff!" This happens through something called HTTP (HyperText Transfer Protocol) or its safer cousin, HTTPS. The server hears the request and responds by shipping over a batch of files—typically an HTML document to start, plus extras like images or stylesheets it might mention.

Step 2: Building the Blueprint (Parsing HTML)

Once the browser gets that HTML file—the backbone of most websites—it starts reading it like a recipe. HTML is full of *tags*, little instructions like <p> for paragraphs or <img> for images, that tell the browser what goes where. The browser parses this code—meaning it breaks it down line by line—and builds a mental map called the DOM, or Document Object Model. Think of the DOM as a family tree of the webpage: the <html> tag is the grandparent, the <body> tag is a parent, and all the headings, text, and pictures are its kids and grandkids. This tree isn't what you see yet—it's just the structure, like a wireframe for a house.

Step 3: Adding Style (Loading CSS)

While the browser's chewing on the HTML, it spots a tag like <link> pointing to a CSS file—the one that controls colors, fonts, and layouts. It grabs that file too and starts matching its rules to the DOM. For example, if the CSS says, "Make all <h1> tags blue and 20 pixels big," the browser tags those instructions onto the right branches of the DOM tree. This step is like picking out paint and furniture for that house—suddenly, it's got personality.

Step 4: Making It Move (Loading JavaScript)

Next up, the browser might find a <script> tag pointing to JavaScript. This is the code that adds interactivity—think dropdown menus, pop-up alerts, or a "like" button that glows when you click it. The browser runs this code, which can tweak the DOM or CSS on the fly. For instance, JavaScript might say, "When someone clicks this button, turn the text red." Unlike HTML and CSS, which are static blueprints, JavaScript is like a live wire—it keeps the page dynamic even after it loads.

Step 5: Painting the Picture (Rendering and Layout)

Now the browser's got the full recipe: the DOM (structure), CSS (style), and maybe some JavaScript (behavior). It's time to turn that into pixels. First, it calculates the *layout*—figuring out where everything sits on the screen. How wide is that header? How much space does this image need? It's like a game of Tetris, fitting every piece into a box based on the screen size and CSS rules. Once the layout's locked in, the browser *paints*—drawing the text, colors, borders, and images onto the canvas of your screen. This happens layer by layer, almost like an artist sketching, inking, and coloring a comic page.

Step 6: Showing It Off

Finally, the browser says, "Ta-da!" and displays the rendered page. If there's JavaScript still at work, it might keep tweaking things—like loading new content as you scroll or popping up a chat window. And if you resize the window or tap a link, parts of this process might kick off again to adjust the view. It's a living, breathing thing, not just a static picture.

Why It's Not Always Instant

Most of the time, this all happens so fast you don't notice. But sometimes you'll hit a slow site—maybe the server's far away, the files are huge, or the code's a mess. Ever seen a page load with text first, then images plopping in late? That's the browser rendering in stages, showing what it's got while it waits for the rest. Big JavaScript files or fancy animations can also bog things down, which is why web developers obsess over making things lean and quick.

The Browser's Secret Sauce

What's wild is that every browser does this a little differently. Chrome uses an engine called Blink, Firefox has Gecko, Safari runs WebKit—each a unique recipe for rendering. They mostly agree on the basics (thanks to web standards), but sometimes a site looks perfect in one browser and wonky in another. It's like how different chefs might bake the same cake with slight twists.

Why This Matters

So why care about rendering? For one, it's the bridge between the coder's brain and your eyes—without it, websites would just be invisible piles of text. Plus, understanding this helps explain the web's quirks: why some pages load slow, why others break on your phone, or why a button might not work until everything's ready. Whether you're just browsing or dreaming of building your own site, knowing how the browser ticks is a superpower.

Next time you click a link, picture that flurry of activity—the request zipping out, the DOM growing, the styles snapping into place, the pixels painting themselves. It's a tiny symphony, conducted in milliseconds, just for you. And as we dig deeper in this book, we'll see how people write the code that makes this magic happen. For now, though, marvel at your browser: it's not just a window—it's a wizard.

Chapter 3
Introduction to HTML5

By now, you've got a handle on what a website is (a digital space packed with stuff) and how browsers turn code into pages (a whirlwind of rendering magic). But what's the glue holding it all together? That's where HTML comes in—the language that tells browsers what to show and how to structure it. And not just any HTML—we're talking HTML5, the latest and greatest version that powers today's web. Think of it as the foundation of a house: it's not the paint or the furniture, but without it, nothing else stands up. Let's dive into what HTML5 is, why it matters, and how it shapes the sites you visit every day.

What's HTML, Anyway?

HTML stands for HyperText Markup Language. "HyperText" is a nod to the web's superpower: linking things together so you can jump from one page to another with a click. "Markup Language" means it's a way to tag and organize content—like putting sticky notes on a book to say, "This is a title," "This is a picture," or "This is a link." It's not a programming language like JavaScript (which makes things move); it's more like a set of instructions for the browser to build the page's skeleton.

HTML has been around since the web's birth in the early 1990s, dreamed up by a guy named Tim Berners-Lee. Back then, it was simple—think black text, blue links, and maybe a blurry photo if you were lucky. Over the years, it grew up through versions like HTML4, adding new tricks along the way. Then, in 2014, HTML5 officially arrived, and it's been the gold standard ever since. Why the big deal? Because HTML5 isn't just an upgrade—it's a revolution that made the web faster, prettier, and way more interactive.

Meet HTML5: The Modern Web's Backbone

So, what's new with HTML5? For starters, it's built for today's internet—not the clunky dial-up days. It's designed to handle everything from basic blogs to video-streaming giants like YouTube. Here's a rundown of what makes HTML5 special:

1. **Better Structure with Semantic Tags**
   Old HTML used generic tags like <div> for everything, leaving browsers and developers to guess what was what. HTML5 introduces *semantic* tags—fancy words for tags with meaning. Think <header> for the top of a page, <footer> for the bottom, <article> for a blog post, or <nav> for a menu. These tags make code cleaner and help browsers (and search engines like Google) understand the page's layout. It's like labeling boxes when you move instead of just tossing stuff in.

2. **Multimedia Without Plugins**
   Remember the days of "Please install Flash to view this video"? HTML5 killed that hassle. With tags like <video> and <audio>, you can embed movies or music directly into a page—no extra software needed. That's why you can watch Netflix or jam to Spotify right in your browser. It's seamless, and it works on your phone, too—no more "This content isn't supported" pop-ups.

3. **Graphics and Animation**
   HTML5 brings the <canvas> tag, a blank slate for drawing shapes, charts, or even games using JavaScript. It also supports SVG (Scalable Vector Graphics), which are crisp, resizable images that don't get pixelated. Together, they let developers create eye-popping visuals without relying on outside tools.

4. **Mobile-Friendly Features**
   The web isn't just for desktops anymore—phones and tablets rule the day. HTML5 was built with that in mind, adding support for touch controls, geolocation (think "Find a café near me"), and offline storage so apps work without Wi-Fi. Ever used Google Maps on the go? Thank HTML5.

5. **Forms That Don't Suck**
   Filling out web forms used to be a chore—clunky and error-prone. HTML5 spruces them up with new input types like <input type="email"> or <input type="date">, plus built-in checks to make sure you typed a real email or picked a valid date. It's small, but it saves headaches.

A Quick HTML5 Example

Let's see it in action. Here's a tiny snippet of HTML5 code for a simple webpage:

```html
<!DOCTYPE html>
<html lang="en">
<head>
  <meta charset="UTF-8">
  <title>My First HTML5 Page</title>
</head>
<body>
    <header>
        <h1>Welcome to My Site</h1>
    </header>
    <main>
        <p>This is a paragraph. Pretty exciting, right?</p>
        <video controls>
            <source src="coolvideo.mp4" type="video/mp4">
            Your browser doesn't support video!
        </video>
    </main>
    <footer>
        <p>© 2025 Me</p>
    </footer>
</body>
</html>
```

What's happening here? The <!DOCTYPE html> line tells the browser, "This is HTML5." The <html> tag wraps everything, with a language attribute (lang="en") for English. Inside <head>, we set the character encoding and title. Then, in <body>, we use semantic tags like <header>, <main>, and <footer> to organize a heading, paragraph, and video. Save this as "index.html," open it in a browser, and you've got a webpage—assuming "coolvideo.mp4" exists!

Why HTML5 Rocks

HTML5 isn't just for coders—it's why the web feels alive today. It's behind the games you play in your browser, the articles you scroll, and the forms you fill out without tearing your hair out. It's also open and universal—any browser worth its salt supports it, from Chrome to Safari. Plus, it's the starting point for anyone who wants to build a site. You don't need to be a tech wizard; with a text editor and some curiosity, you can write HTML5 and see results in minutes.

Where We're Going Next

This is just the tip of the iceberg. HTML5 is the foundation, but it teams up with CSS (for style) and JavaScript (for action) to make websites sing. In the chapters ahead, we'll explore how those pieces fit together, how to write your own HTML5, and what makes a site not just functional but unforgettable. For now, picture HTML5 as the web's trusty architect—quietly shaping everything you see, one tag at a time.

Chapter 4
Choosing a Text Editor
(VS Code, Sublime Text, etc.)

You've got the basics down: websites live on servers, browsers render them, and HTML5 is the foundation. Now it's time to roll up your sleeves and start building something yourself. But before you write a single line of code, you need a tool—a text editor. Think of it as your digital workbench, where you'll craft HTML, CSS, and JavaScript into webpages. The good news? There are tons of great options out there, from freebies to fancy ones, each with its own vibe. The tricky part? Picking one that fits you. Let's explore some of the heavy hitters—Visual Studio Code, Sublime Text, and a few others—so you can find your perfect match.

What's a Text Editor, Anyway?

A text editor is just a program for writing and editing plain text—like the stuff that makes up HTML files. It's not Word or Google Docs (those add formatting you don't want); it's leaner, meaner, and built for code. A good editor highlights syntax (making tags like <p> stand out), catches typos, and speeds up your workflow. Some are simple, others are packed with features—it's about what clicks for you. Here's a rundown of the top contenders.

Visual Studio Code (VS Code)

- **What It Is**: Made by Microsoft, VS Code is the rockstar of text editors—free, open-source, and ridiculously popular. It's like a Swiss Army knife for coding.

- **Why It's Great**: Out of the box, it's got syntax highlighting, auto-complete (it guesses what you're typing), and a built-in terminal to test stuff. But the real magic? Extensions. Want HTML snippets, a live preview of your webpage, or a dark theme that's easy on the eyes? There's an extension for that. It's also lightweight for a powerhouse, running smooth on Windows, Mac, or Linux.

- **Downsides**: It can feel overwhelming at first—too many menus and options. And if you pile on extensions, it might slow down on older machines.

- **Who It's For**: Beginners who want room to grow, or anyone who loves customizing their tools. It's a safe bet for most.

Sublime Text

- **What It Is**: Sublime Text is the sleek, speedy veteran—around since 2008, with a loyal fanbase. It's not free ($99 for a license), but you can try it indefinitely with a nag screen.

- **Why It's Great**: It's fast—like, *blink-and-it's-open* fast. The interface is clean, with a distraction-free mode that's perfect for focusing. It's got powerful features like "Goto Anything" (jump to any file or line instantly) and multi-line editing (change 10 things at once). Plugins add extras like VS Code's extensions, though they're less central to the experience.

- **Downsides**: That price tag stings for a beginner, and it's less hand-holding than VS Code—no built-in terminal or live preview without tweaking. The community's smaller, too, so updates are slower.

- **Who It's For**: People who value speed and simplicity over bells and whistles, or pros who don't mind paying for quality.

Notepad++ (Windows Only)

- **What It Is**: A free, no-frills editor that's been a Windows staple for years. It's basic but gets the job done.

- **Why It's Great**: It's lightweight and opens instantly, even on ancient PCs. It supports syntax highlighting for HTML and tons of other languages, plus handy tricks like search-and-replace across multiple files. No install fuss—just download and go.

- **Downsides**: It's Windows-only (sorry, Mac and Linux folks), and the interface looks dated. No built-in terminal or fancy extensions—it's bare-bones compared to VS Code.

- **Who It's For**: Absolute beginners on a budget, or anyone with an old Windows laptop who just wants to dip their toes in.

Atom

- **What It Is**: Another free, open-source editor, built by GitHub (now owned by Microsoft). It's like VS Code's artsy cousin.

- **Why It's Great**: It's customizable with themes and packages, and it integrates nicely with Git (a tool for tracking code changes). The interface is friendly, with split-screen editing for juggling files.

- **Downsides**: It's slower than VS Code or Sublime—startup can lag, and big projects might chug. It's also less actively developed since VS Code stole its thunder.

- **Who It's For**: People who like a hacker vibe and don't mind a slightly heavier tool, or those already using GitHub.

Bonus: Online Editors (CodePen, Replit)

- **What They Are**: Web-based tools where you can code right in your browser—no downloads needed.

- **Why They're Great**: Instant setup, perfect for testing HTML5 snippets or sharing ideas. CodePen shines for front-end experiments (HTML/CSS/JavaScript), with live previews. Replit's broader, supporting full projects and collaboration.

- **Downsides**: You need internet, and they're less robust for big sites. Local backups are trickier, too.

- **Who They're For**: Beginners wanting to play without installing anything, or pros prototyping on the fly.

How to Choose

So, which one's "best"? It depends. If you're new and want free power, start with VS Code—it's got tutorials galore and grows with you. If speed's your jam and you've got cash, try Sublime Text. On a tight budget or old machine? Notepad++ or an online editor like CodePen works. Here's a quick checklist:

- **Free or paid?** VS Code and Notepad++ are free; Sublime costs.

- **Beginner or pro?** VS Code and Atom ease you in; Sublime assumes you know a bit.

- **Fast or feature-packed?** Sublime's lean; VS Code's loaded.

- **Local or online?** Most are local; CodePen's cloud-based.

Getting Started

Pick one, download it (or open it online), and try typing that HTML5 example from Chapter 3. Watch the colors pop as syntax highlighting kicks in—it's your first taste of coding life. Don't stress about mastering it yet; just get comfy. You can always switch later—tools are like shoes, and you'll find the pair that fits.

Next up, we'll take your editor for a spin and write some real HTML5. For now, choose your weapon, install it, and get ready to build. The web's waiting for your mark!

Chapter 5
Installing a Browser for Testing

You've got your text editor locked and loaded, ready to write some HTML5 magic. But here's the catch: code doesn't mean much until you see it in action. That's where a web browser comes in—not just for scrolling social media or shopping, but as your testing ground. In Chapter 2, we saw how browsers render websites, turning tags into pixels. Now, it's time to install one (or a few) to test your own creations. Don't worry—it's easier than it sounds, and it's your ticket to making sure your site looks and works the way you want. Let's get you set up.

Why Test in a Browser?

Before we dive in, why bother installing browsers specifically for testing? Can't you just use the one you've already got? Sure, you could—but web development's tricky. Different browsers (Chrome, Firefox, Safari, etc.) render pages slightly differently, thanks to their unique engines (Blink, Gecko, WebKit). A button that's perfect in Chrome might vanish in Firefox, or an animation might stutter on an old phone. Testing across browsers helps you catch these quirks early, so your site shines for everyone, not just you. Plus, browsers come with developer tools—secret menus to peek at your code, tweak it live, and spot errors. Installing a few now saves headaches later.

Step 1: Pick Your Browsers

You don't need every browser under the sun, but a small posse covers most bases. Here's a starter lineup:

- **Google Chrome**: The king of browsers—fast, popular, and packed with dev tools. Its Blink engine powers other big names like Edge and Opera, so testing here checks a lot of boxes.

- **Mozilla Firefox**: Open-source and privacy-focused, with a Gecko engine that's different enough from Chrome to catch oddities. Its dev tools are top-notch, too.

- **Microsoft Edge**: Pre-installed on Windows, it's now Blink-based (like Chrome) but worth a look for Windows users.

- **Safari**: Mac's default, running WebKit. Essential if you're targeting iPhone or iPad users, though it's Mac-only.

- **Bonus: Mobile Browsers**: Chrome and Safari on your phone mimic how most people browse today.

For beginners, Chrome and Firefox are a killer duo—widely used, developer-friendly, and free. Add others as you grow.

Step 2: Check What You've Got

First, see what's already on your machine. On Windows, Edge is built-in; Macs have Safari. Chrome or Firefox might be there if you've browsed before. Open them, type "about:version" in the address bar, and check the version number. If it's old (say, over a year behind), update it—old browsers miss modern HTML5 features. To update:

- **Chrome**: Click the three dots (top right) > Help > About Google Chrome. It'll fetch the latest.

- **Firefox**: Menu (three lines, top right) > Help > About Firefox. Updates download automatically.

- **Edge/Safari**: Usually tied to system updates—check your OS settings.

Step 3: Install Fresh Browsers

Need a new one? Here's how to grab Chrome and Firefox (tweak for others):

- **Google Chrome**:

  1. Go to www.google.com/chrome in your current browser.

  2. Hit "Download Chrome," pick your OS (Windows, Mac, Linux), and run the installer.

  3. Open it after install—pin it to your dock or taskbar for quick access.

- **Mozilla Firefox**:

  1. Visit www.mozilla.org/firefox in your current browser.

  2. Click "Download Firefox," choose your OS, and run the file.

  3. Launch it and keep it handy.

Both are free, take minutes to install, and don't mess with your existing setup. Pro tip: install them in separate folders if you want multiple versions (like a beta build) for extra testing.

Step 4: Test Your First Page

Got your browsers? Let's try them out. Open that HTML5 example from Chapter 3 (or write a quick <p>Hello, world!</p> in a file called "test. html"). Save it somewhere easy, like your desktop. Then:

1. Right-click the file and choose "Open with" > Chrome (or Firefox).

2. Watch your words appear! Switch browsers—does it look the same?

3. Or drag the file into an open browser window—same deal.

If it works, congrats—you've just tested your first webpage! If not (say, it's blank), double-check your code—typos sneak in.

Step 5: Explore Developer Tools

Browsers aren't just viewers—they're debuggers. Open your page, then:

- **Chrome**: Right-click anywhere > "Inspect" (or Ctrl+Shift+I / Cmd+Opt+I). A panel pops up showing the HTML and CSS.

- **Firefox**: Right-click > "Inspect" (or Ctrl+Shift+E). Similar deal, with a slick layout view.

- Tweak a color or tag in the tools—see it change live. It's like X-ray vision for your site.

These tools show the DOM (remember Chapter 2?), errors, and more. Play around—you can't break anything permanently.

Tips for Testing

- **Keep Them Updated**: New versions fix bugs and add HTML5 goodies.

- **Test Early, Test Often**: Check your code after every big change.

- **Go Mobile**: Open your page on your phone's browser—half the web's traffic is mobile now.

- **Don't Panic**: Differences between browsers are normal—we'll tackle fixes later.

Why This Matters

Installing browsers for testing isn't just setup—it's your first step into a developer's mindset. You're not just writing code; you're crafting experiences for real people on real devices. Chrome might be your daily driver, but Firefox might catch a glitch your visitors would see. Plus, those dev tools? They're your cheat codes for learning and fixing as you go.

Chapter 6
Folder Structure for Your Project

You've got your text editor humming, your browsers ready to test, and maybe even a little HTML5 under your belt. Now it's time to set up your workspace—like clearing a desk before a big project. In web development, that means creating a folder structure: a neat, logical way to store your files so you don't lose track of your HTML, CSS, images, and whatever else you're cooking up. It might sound boring compared to writing code, but trust me—a good setup saves you from chaos later. Let's break it down and build a foundation for your first web project.

Why Bother with Folders?

Picture this: you're working on a site with a homepage, some pictures, and a stylesheet. At first, it's just three files—easy to manage on your desktop. But then you add a blog page, a contact form, some JavaScript, and a dozen more images. Suddenly, it's a mess—files everywhere, names like "image1.jpg" and "newfile.html" that make no sense. A smart folder structure keeps things tidy, speeds up your workflow, and makes it easier to test and share your project. Plus, it mimics how real websites are organized on servers, so you're learning pro habits from the start.

The Basic Recipe

For most small web projects, a simple structure works wonders. Here's a starter kit you can copy:

- **project-folder/** (name it whatever—like "my-first-site")
  - **index.html** (your homepage)
  - **css/** (a folder for styles)
    - **style.css** (your main stylesheet)
  - **js/** (a folder for JavaScript)
    - **script.js** (your main script file)
  - **images/** (a folder for pictures)
    - **logo.png**

- **hero.jpg**
  - **docs/** (optional, for notes or PDFs)
    - **plan.txt**

This setup splits your stuff into categories: HTML for structure, CSS for style, JavaScript for interactivity, and images for visuals. The root folder ("project-folder") holds everything, and "index.html" is the entry point—browsers look for it first when you open the folder or host it online.

How It Works

Let's say you've got this structure. In your "index.html," you'd link to the other files like this:

```
<link rel="stylesheet" href="css/style.css">

<script src="js/script.js"></script>

<img src="images/logo.png" alt="My Logo">
```

The paths ("css/style.css") tell the browser where to find each file relative to "index.html." Keep it organized, and these links stay simple—no hunting through a cluttered pile.

Step-by-Step Setup

Ready to make it? Here's how:

1. **Pick a Spot**: Choose a location on your computer—like "Documents" or "Desktop." Create a new folder called "my-first-site" (or whatever inspires you).

2. **Add the Basics**: Inside, make a file called "index.html" (use your text editor—save it with a ".html" extension). Then create subfolders: "css," "js," and "images." Right-click > New Folder works, or use your editor's sidebar if it has one (VS Code does).

3. **Fill It Up**: In "css," add "style.css." In "js," add "script.js." Drop a couple images (like a logo or a photo) into "images." For now, they can be empty—test files to play with.

4. **Test It**: Open "index.html" in a browser (right-click > Open with Chrome). Add some HTML—like <h1>Hello from my site!</h1>—save, and refresh. It's alive!

Naming Rules

A quick word on names: keep them clear and consistent. Use lower-case (browsers sometimes trip on capitals), no spaces (use "my-file" not "my file"), and stick to letters, numbers, dashes, or underscores. "style.css" beats "My Cool Style Sheet.css" every time—short, readable, and web-friendly.

Scaling Up

This basic structure works for small sites, but what if your project grows? Here's how it might evolve:

- **Multiple Pages**: Add "about.html" or "contact.html" in the root next to "index.html."

- **More Styles**: Split "css" into "base.css" (core styles) and "homepage.css" (page-specific).

- **Assets**: Add "fonts" or "videos" folders alongside "images."

- **Big Projects**: Group related files—like "blog/index.html" and "blog/style.css"—in subfolders.

For now, though, the simple setup is plenty. Start small, and let your structure grow with your skills.

Why It's a Big Deal

A good folder structure isn't just about neatness—it's practical. When you test in browsers (like we set up in Chapter 5), you'll drag "index.html" into Chrome or Firefox, and it'll pull everything else along if the paths are right. Later, when you upload to a web server, this layout matches how hosting works—no surprises. Plus, if you share your project (say, with a friend or teacher), they'll find their way around without a treasure map.

Tips to Keep It Smooth

- **Stay Consistent**: Name "css" the same across projects—habits save time.

- **Backup**: Copy your folder to a USB or cloud (like Google Drive) now and then.

- **Test Early**: Open "index.html" after every big change—catch broken links fast.

- **Keep It Lean**: Don't hoard old files—delete what you don't need.

Chapter 7
Anatomy of an HTML Document

You've got your project folder set up, your text editor humming, and your browsers ready to roll. Now it's time to dissect the star of the show: the HTML document. Think of it as the blueprint for every webpage—a simple text file that tells the browser what to display and how it's structured. In Chapter 3, we peeked at HTML5 and threw together a quick example. Here, we'll break it down piece by piece, so you know exactly what's happening under the hood. By the end, you'll be ready to build your own pages with confidence. Let's cut it open and explore!

The Big Picture

An HTML document is just a plain text file with a ".html" extension—like "index.html." Inside, it's a mix of *tags* (instructions in angle brackets, like <p>) and *content* (the stuff you see, like text or images). Tags work in pairs—<p> to start a paragraph, </p> to end it—wrapping content like bookends. Together, they form *elements*, the building blocks of your page. The browser reads this file top to bottom, turning tags into a visible layout via the DOM (remember Chapter 2?). Every HTML document follows a standard anatomy, and HTML5 keeps it clean and modern. Here's what it looks like.

The Skeleton: A Full Example

Let's start with a complete HTML5 document, then unpack it:

```
<!DOCTYPE html>
<html lang="en">
<head>
    <meta charset="UTF-8">
    <title>My Awesome Page</title>
    <link rel="stylesheet" href="css/style.css">
</head>
<body>
```

```
    <header>
        <h1>Welcome to My Site</h1>
    </header>
    <main>
        <p>This is my first webpage. Pretty cool, huh?</p>
        <img src="images/cat.jpg" alt="A fluffy cat">
    </main>
    <footer>
        <p>&copy; 2025 Me</p>
    </footer>
    <script src="js/script.js"></script>
</body>
</html>
```

Save this as "index.html" in your project folder (from Chapter 6), open it in a browser, and you'll see a basic page. Now, let's dissect each part.

1. <!DOCTYPE html>: The Declaration

This line isn't a tag—it's a shout to the browser: "Hey, I'm an HTML5 document!" It's required at the top, telling the browser to expect modern HTML rules. Skip it, and older browsers might get confused, rendering your page in "quirks mode" (a messy throwback setting). Keep it simple—it's always the same.

2. <html>: The Root Element

The <html> tag wraps everything else, like the cover of a book. It's the root of the DOM tree, and every other element lives inside it. The lang="en" attribute says the page is in English (swap "en" for "es" for Spanish, etc.), helping screen readers and search engines. It closes with </html> at the bottom.

3. <head>: The Brain

The <head> section is like the page's control room—it holds info *about* the page, not what you see. It's invisible to users but critical for browsers. Inside, you'll find:

1. **<meta charset="UTF-8">**: Sets the character encoding to UTF-8, a universal standard that handles letters, emojis, and more. Without

it, special characters (like © or ñ) might turn into gibberish.

2. **<title>**: The page's name—here, "My Awesome Page." It shows up in the browser tab and bookmarks. Keep it short and descriptive.

3. **<link>**: Connects external files, like "css/style.css" for styles. The href points to the file's path (relative to "index.html").

You can add more here later—like icons or extra metadata—but this is the core.

4. <body>: The Heart

The <body> is where the action happens—it's everything users see and interact with. If <head> is the brain, <body> is the face, arms, and legs. Inside ours:

1. **<header>**: A semantic tag (HTML5's gift) for the top section—here, a heading with <h1>.

2. **<main>**: The meat of the page—text in <p> (paragraph) and an <img> for a cat pic. The src attribute links to "images/cat.jpg," and alt describes it for accessibility (screen readers love this).

3. **<footer>**: The bottom bit—here, a copyright notice with © (a special code for ©).

4. **<script>**: Loads "js/script.js" for interactivity. Put it at the end of <body> so the page loads first, then the script kicks in.

How It Fits Together

The browser reads this top-down: <!DOCTYPE> sets the rules, <html> starts the tree, <head> preps the metadata, and <body> delivers the goods. Each element nests inside another—like Russian dolls—forming a hierarchy the browser renders into a webpage. Open it in Chrome's developer tools (right-click > Inspect), and you'll see the DOM match this structure perfectly.

Why It Matters

Understanding this anatomy isn't just trivia—it's power. You control what the browser shows by arranging these pieces. Mess up a tag (forget a </p>), and the page might break. Nail it, and you've got a solid foundation for CSS and JavaScript to jazz up. Plus, HTML5's semantic tags (<header>, <main>) make your code readable—to you, collaborators, and search engines.

Play with It

Take this example, tweak it in your text editor, and test it in your browsers (Chapter 5). Change the <title>, swap the <p> text, or point <img> to a real photo in your "images" folder. Save, refresh, and watch it update— your first hands-on HTML win!

Chapter 8
HTML5 Doctype and Document Structure

Last chapter, we sliced open an HTML document and poked around its guts—tags, elements, and the <head>-<body> split. Now, let's zoom in on two big pieces we breezed past: the HTML5 doctype and the document's overall structure. These might sound like dry technicalities, but they're the backbone of every webpage you'll build. The doctype tells the browser what rules to play by, and the structure keeps your code organized and predictable. Nail these, and you're set to create pages that work everywhere. Let's dig in and see how they shape your HTML5 projects.

The Doctype: Setting the Stage

Every HTML5 document starts with this little line:

```
<!DOCTYPE html>
```

It's not a tag—no angle brackets here—but it's non-negotiable. Think of it as the opening whistle in a game: it tells the browser, "This is HTML5, so render it with the latest, greatest standards." Without it, browsers might fall back to "quirks mode"—an old, messy way of guessing how to display pages from the wild-west days of the web (think 1990s chaos). Quirks mode can twist your layout, break CSS, or make modern features like <video> stumble. With <!DOCTYPE html>, you're saying, "No guessing—follow HTML5 rules."

The beauty? It's dead simple. Unlike older versions (HTML4 or XHTML had clunky doctypes with long strings of gibberish), HTML5 keeps it short and sweet. No matter the project—small page or sprawling site—it's always <!DOCTYPE html>, case-insensitive, at the very top. Try skipping it in your "index.html" and testing in Chrome—things might still *look* okay, but under the hood, it's a gamble.

The Document Structure: A Reliable Frame

Once the doctype's in place, your HTML5 document follows a standard structure—a skeleton that holds everything together. It's like the frame of a house: consistent, logical, and ready for you to fill in. Here's the full rundown, using the example from Chapter 7 with a few tweaks:

```html
<!DOCTYPE html>
<html lang="en">
<head>
    <meta charset="UTF-8">
    <meta name="viewport" content="width=device-width, ini-
tial-scale=1.0">
    <title>My HTML5 Structure</title>
    <link rel="stylesheet" href="css/style.css">
</head>
<body>
    <header>
        <h1>My Site Rocks</h1>
        <nav>
            <a href="index.html">Home</a>
            <a href="about.html">About</a>
        </nav>
    </header>
    <main>
        <section>
            <h2>Main Content</h2>
            <p>This is where the good stuff lives.</p>
        </section>
    </main>
    <footer>
        <p>Built with HTML5, 2025</p>
    </footer>
    <script src="js/script.js"></script>
</body>
</html>
```

Let's break it into its core chunks and see why they matter.

My Site Rocks

Home About

Main Content

This is where the good stuff lives.

Built with HTML5, 2025

---

1. <html>: The Container

The <html> tag wraps the whole document (after the doctype), acting as the root element. The lang="en" attribute signals the language—English here—which helps accessibility tools (like screen readers) and search engines. Everything nests inside <html> and ends with </html>. It's the outer shell, holding the <head> and <body>.

2. <head>: The Metadata Hub

The <head> is the behind-the-scenes boss. It's not visible on the page but tells the browser how to handle it. Key players:

- **<meta charset="UTF-8">**: Ensures text (letters, symbols, emojis) displays correctly across devices.

- **<meta name="viewport">**: A mobile must-have—width=device-width, initial-scale=1.0 makes your page scale nicely on phones and tablets. Skip it, and your site might look tiny on a screen.

- **<title>**: Names your page for tabs and bookmarks.

- **<link>**: Hooks up your CSS file (from your "css" folder).

This section's small but mighty—think of it as the instruction manual for the browser.

3. <body>: The Visible Stuff

The <body> is where your content lives—everything users see and touch. HTML5's semantic tags shine here:

- **<header>**: The top section—here with a heading (<h1>) and navigation (<nav> with links).

- **<main>**: The heart of the page, wrapping core content like a <section> with text.

- **<footer>**: The bottom, often for credits or links.

- **<script>**: Loads JavaScript at the end, so the page renders first.

These semantic tags (new in HTML5) aren't just fancy—they tell browsers, search engines, and screen readers what each part *means*, not just how it looks.

Why This Structure Rules

This setup—doctype plus <html>, <head>, <body>—is the HTML5 standard for a reason. It's predictable: every page you build can follow this pattern, so you're not reinventing the wheel. It's flexible: add more sections, scripts, or styles as needed. And it's future-proof: HTML5's simplicity and semantics play nice with modern tools and devices. Test this in your browsers (Chapter 5), and you'll see it render cleanly—tweak it, and it still holds up.

Try It Out

Open your text editor, paste this code into "index.html" (in your project folder from Chapter 6), and save. Open it in Chrome or Firefox—boom, a structured page! Add a "css/style.css" file with h1 { color: blue; }, save, and refresh—your <h1> turns blue. You're wiring it together, piece by piece.

Chapter 9
Basic HTML Tags
(\<html\>, \<head\>, \<body\>, etc.)

You've got the HTML5 doctype locked down and a solid document structure in place. Now it's time to meet the core crew: the basic HTML tags that show up in every webpage. These are the building blocks—like Lego pieces—that shape your content and tell the browser what's what. Last chapter, we saw them in action; here, we'll get to know them up close, starting with the big three—\<html\>, \<head\>, and \<body\>—and adding a few friends to the mix. By the end, you'll wield these tags like a pro, ready to stack them into pages of your own. Let's jump in!

The Core Trio: \<html\>, \<head\>, and \<body\>

Every HTML document leans on these three tags—they're the frame everything else hangs on. Here's what they do, with a fresh example to play with:

```
<!DOCTYPE html>
<html lang="en">
<head>
    <meta charset="UTF-8">
    <title>Hello World</title>
</head>
<body>
  <p>This is my page. Hi there!</p>
</body>
</html>
```

1. \<html\>: The Root Tag

- **What It Does**: The \<html\> tag is the container for your entire document—everything (except the doctype) lives between \<html\> and \</html\>. It's the top of the DOM tree (Chapter 2), the starting point for the browser's rendering.

- **Key Attribute**: lang="en" sets the language (English here), helping accessibility tools and search engines. Swap "en" for "fr" (French) or "ja" (Japanese) as needed.

- **Why It Matters**: Without it, your page isn't valid HTML—browsers might still render it, but it's a sloppy foundation.

2. <head>: The Control Center

- **What It Does**: The <head> tag holds metadata—info about the page that doesn't show up directly. It's like the backstage crew, setting up the show.

- **Common Kids**:

    - <meta charset="UTF-8">: Ensures text displays right (accents, emojis, etc.).

    - <title>: Names your page—here, "Hello World"—showing in the browser tab.

- **Why It Matters**: It preps the browser and connects external files (like CSS with <link>). Skip it, and your page might load wonky or lack a title.

3. <body>: The Showroom

- **What It Does**: The <body> tag is where the visible stuff lives—text, images, buttons, all the goodies users see and interact with.

- **Example**: <p>This is my page. Hi there!</p> puts a paragraph onscreen.

- **Why It Matters**: No <body>, no content—your page would be a blank stare. It's the heart of your site.

The Supporting Cast: Basic Content Tags

These tags live inside <body> (sometimes <head>), adding meat to your page. Let's meet a few essentials:

```
<!DOCTYPE html>
<html lang="en">
<head>
    <meta charset="UTF-8">
    <title>My First Tags</title>
</head>
```

```
<body>
    <h1>This is a Big Heading</h1>
    <p>Here's some text. <strong>Bold stuff</strong> is cool.</p>
    <a href="https://example.com">Click me!</a>
    <img src="images/dog.jpg" alt="A happy dog">
</body>
</html>
```

4. *<h1> to <h6>: Headings*

- **What They Do**: These tags create headings, from <h1> (biggest, most important) to <h6> (smallest). They're like chapter titles in a book.

- **Example**: <h1>This is a Big Heading</h1>—great for page titles.

- **Why They Matter**: They structure your content (think SEO and accessibility) and grab attention. Use <h1> once per page, then <h2>, <h3>, etc., for subheadings.

5. *<p>: Paragraphs*

- **What It Does**: The <p> tag wraps blocks of text—your story, info, or ramblings.

- **Example**: <p>Here's some text.</p>—simple but vital.

- **Why It Matters**: It's the workhorse of content, spacing text nicely for readability. Nest other tags (like <strong>) inside for emphasis.

6. <a>: Links

- **What It Does**: The <a> tag (for "anchor") creates hyperlinks—clickable bridges to other pages or sites.

- **Key Attribute**: href="https://example.com" sets the destination.

- **Example**: <a href="https://example.com">Click me!</a>—words become a portal.

- **Why It Matters**: It's the "hyper" in HyperText—linking is the web's soul.

7. <img>: Images

- **What It Does**: The <img> tag embeds pictures—no closing tag needed (it's *self-closing*).

- **Key Attributes**: src="images/dog.jpg" points to the file; alt="A happy dog" describes it for screen readers or if the image fails.

- **Example**: <img src="images/dog.jpg" alt="A happy dog">.

- **Why It Matters**: Visuals spice up your page, and alt keeps it accessible.

8. <strong> and <em>: Emphasis

- **What They Do**: <strong> makes text bold (important stuff); <em> italicizes it (emphasis or tone).

- **Example**: <p><strong>Bold stuff</strong> is cool.</p>—stands out.

- **Why They Matter**: They add flavor to text without needing CSS yet—semantic and simple.

How They Work Together

These tags nest like a family tree: <html> holds <head> and <body>, <body> holds <h1>, <p>, etc. The browser reads them in order, rendering a page with a title (from <head>), a heading, text, a link, and an image (from <body>). Test this in your project folder (Chapter 6)—save it as "index.html," open it in Chrome, and tweak it. Swap the <h1> text or link—see it update live.

Why These Tags Rock

They're basic but powerful—every site, from blogs to Amazon, uses them. They're HTML5-ready, universal across browsers, and easy to learn. Start with these, and you've got a page that's structured, clickable, and visual— no fancy code required.

Hands-On Time

Open your text editor, type this example, and save it in your "my-first-site" folder. Add an image to "images/" (grab one online if needed), then test it in your browsers (Chapter 5). Play—change the <title>, add another <p>, or link to "about.html" (even if it's empty). You're building real pages now!

Chapter 10
Comments in HTML

You've got the core HTML tags down—<html>, <head>, <body>, and friends—and you're starting to build pages that actually do stuff. But as your code grows, it can get messy or hard to follow, especially if you step away and come back later. Enter HTML comments: little notes you tuck into your code that the browser ignores but you (and others) can read. Think of them as sticky notes for your project—handy for reminders, explanations, or just keeping things sane. Let's explore how they work, why they're useful, and how to sprinkle them into your HTML5 documents.

What Are HTML Comments?

In HTML, a comment is a snippet of text that's invisible on the webpage but visible in the code. It's there for humans—developers like you—not the browser. Comments don't affect how your page looks or works; they're purely for organization and clarity. Here's what one looks like:

```
<!-- This is a comment -->
```

The magic happens between <!-- and -->. Anything inside those markers—words, numbers, even gibberish—gets skipped by the browser when rendering. It's that simple.

How to Write Them

Let's see comments in action with a basic page:

```
<!DOCTYPE html>
<html lang="en">
<head>
    <meta charset="UTF-8">
    <title>My Commented Page</title>
    <!-- Link to my stylesheet -->
```

```
    <link rel="stylesheet" href="css/style.css">
</head>
<body>
    <!-- Main heading for the page -->
    <h1>Welcome to My Site</h1>
    <p>This is some text.</p>
    <!-- Image of my dog, added March 2025 -->
    <img src="images/dog.jpg" alt="My dog">
    <!-- TODO: Add more content later -->
</body>
</html>
```

Open this in a browser, and you'll see the heading, text, and image—no trace of the comments. But in your text editor (Chapter 4), they're there, guiding you like a map.

The Rules

- **Start and End**: Always use <!-- to begin and --> to end. Miss one, and your page might break (or hide stuff accidentally).

- **Anywhere's Fair Game**: Put comments in <head>, <body>, or between tags—just not *inside* a tag (e.g., <p <!-- nope --> won't work).

- **No Nesting**: You can't put a comment inside another comment—<!-- Outer <!-- Inner --> --> confuses the browser.

Why Use Comments?

Comments might feel like extra work, but they're a lifesaver. Here's why they matter:

1. **Memory Joggers**: <p>I wrote this!</p> <!-- Added on March 4, 2025 -->—months later, you'll know when and why.

2. **Teamwork**: If you share your code (say, with a friend or teacher), <!-- Navigation links go here --> explains your plan.

3. **Debugging**: Temporarily "hide" code without deleting it—comment out a line:

```
<!-- <p>This won't show up</p> -->
```

Refresh your browser—it's gone, but still there when you need it back.

4. **Planning**: Mark spots for future work—<!-- TODO: Add contact form -->—like a to-do list in your code.

Real-World Examples

Here's a beefier example to see comments in context:

```
<!DOCTYPE html>
<html lang="en">
<head>
    <!-- Character encoding and viewport for mobile -->
    <meta charset="UTF-8">
    <meta name="viewport" content="width=device-width, ini-
tial-scale=1.0">
    <title>My Project</title>
</head>
<body>
    <!-- Site header with logo and nav -->
    <header>
        <h1>My Project</h1>
        <!-- Navigation links, update as pages are added -->
        <nav>
            <a href="index.html">Home</a>
            <a href="about.html">About</a>
        </nav>
    </header>
    <!-- Main content section -->
    <main>
        <p>Welcome to my site! More coming soon.</p>
        <!-- Temporary placeholder image -->
```

```
        <img src="images/placeholder.jpg" alt="Placeholder">
    </main>
    <!-- Footer with copyright -->
    <footer>
        <p>© 2025 Me</p>
    </footer>
</body>
</html>
```

index.html

Home About

Welcome to my site! More coming soon.

© 2025 Me

Comments here label sections, explain choices, and flag temporary bits. It's cleaner and easier to navigate—especially if your project grows.

Try It Out

Open your "index.html" from Chapter 9 in your text editor (like VS Code). Add some comments:

- Above \<h1\>, write \<!-- My main title -->.

- After <p>, add <!-- Add more text later -->.

- Comment out <img> with <!-- and -->—watch it vanish in your browser (Chapter 5), then uncomment it to bring it back.

Save, refresh in Chrome or Firefox, and see how the comments stay hidden but useful. Play around—label your tags or jot a note about your next step.

Tips for Smart Commenting

- **Keep It Short**: <!-- Header --> beats a novel—save space and time.

- **Be Clear**: <!-- Links to social media --> is better than <!-- Stuff here -->.

- **Don't Overdo It**: Comment key spots, not every line—too many clog the view.

- **Update Them**: If you change code, tweak the comments—stale notes confuse more than help.

Why Comments Are Your Friend

Comments don't make your page prettier, but they make *you* better. They're a habit pros swear by—keeping code readable, debuggable, and shareable. As your projects get bigger (think multiple pages or collaborators), comments turn chaos into order. Plus, they're free—zero cost for a big payoff.

Chapter 11
Semantic HTML5 Elements
(\<header\>, \<main\>, \<section\>,
\<article\>, \<footer\>, etc.)

You've mastered the basic HTML tags and learned to leave yourself notes with comments. Now, let's level up with HTML5's secret weapon: semantic elements. These tags—like \<header\>, \<main\>, \<section\>, \<article\>, and \<footer\>—aren't just fancy names; they're smarter versions of the old \<div\> tag, giving your page structure *and* meaning. They tell browsers, search engines, and screen readers what each part of your site is for, not just how it looks. By the end of this chapter, you'll wield these tags to build pages that are cleaner, more accessible, and future-proof. Let's dive into the semantic revolution!

What's "Semantic" Mean?

In HTML, "semantic" means "having meaning." Old-school HTML used \<div\> for everything—headers, footers, content—leaving browsers to guess what was what. HTML5 fixes that with tags that describe their purpose. Think of it like labeling boxes when you move: \<header\> says "top stuff," \<main\> says "core content," \<footer\> says "bottom bits." This clarity isn't just for you—it helps search engines rank your site and assistive tech (like screen readers) navigate it for users with disabilities.

The Semantic Stars

Here's a rundown of the key players, with an example to see them in action:

```
<!DOCTYPE html>

<html lang="en">

<head>

    <meta charset="UTF-8">

    <title>My Semantic Site</title>
```

```html
    <!-- Stylesheet link -->
    <link rel="stylesheet" href="css/style.css">
</head>
<body>
    <!-- Site header with branding -->
    <header>
        <h1>My Blog</h1>
        <nav>
            <a href="index.html">Home</a>
            <a href="about.html">About</a>
        </nav>
    </header>

    <!-- Main content area -->
    <main>
        <!-- Blog post section -->
        <section>
            <h2>Latest News</h2>
            <article>
                <h3>Post Title</h3>
                <p>A short teaser about today's topic.</p>
            </article>
            <article>
                <h3>Another Post</h3>
                <p>More exciting stuff here.</p>
            </article>
        </section>
    </main>

    <!-- Footer with extra info -->
    <footer>
```

```
        <p>© 2025 Me | Contact: me@example.com</p>
    </footer>
  </body>
</html>
```

Save this as "index.html" in your project folder (Chapter 6), open it in a browser (Chapter 5), and you've got a semantic page. Let's break down each tag.

1. <header>: The Top Dog

- **What It Does**: Marks the introductory or navigational part of a page—or even a section. Think logos, titles, or menus.

- **Example**: <header><h1>My Blog</h1></header>—a site-wide banner.

- **Why It's Cool**: It's clearer than a <div class="header">, and you can use it multiple times (e.g., inside an <article> for a post header).

2. <main>: The Heart

- **What It Does**: Wraps the primary content—the stuff your page is *about*. Only one <main> per page, please.

- **Example**: <main><p>Welcome!</p></main>—the core goods.

- **Why It's Cool**: Screen readers jump here first, skipping fluff, and search engines prioritize it.

3. <section>: The Organizer

- **What It Does**: Groups related content, like a chapter or topic. It's a chunk with a purpose, often with a heading.

- **Example**: <section><h2>News</h2><p>Stuff happens.</p></section>—a themed block.

- **Why It's Cool**: It divides <main> into digestible parts, making long pages less overwhelming.

4. <article>: The Standalone

- **What It Does**: Holds content that makes sense on its own—like a blog post, news story, or review. It's reusable elsewhere.

- **Example**: <article><h3>Post Title</h3><p>Text</p></article>—a mini-page.

- **Why It's Cool**: Perfect for blogs or feeds—search engines love it, and it's portable.

- **What It Does**: Caps off a page or section with extras—copyrights, links, or contact info.

- **Example**: <footer><p>© 2025 Me</p></footer>—the sign-off.

- **Why It's Cool**: It's a natural endcap, and like <header>, it can live in smaller sections too.

Bonus: <nav> and <aside>

- **<nav>**: Wraps navigation links—<nav><a href="index.html">Home</a></nav>. It flags menus for accessibility.

- **<aside>**: Holds side content—like a sidebar or fun fact—<aside><p>Trivia!</p></aside>. It's related but not essential.

Why Semantic Tags Win

These tags don't *look* different from <div> out of the box—add CSS (coming soon) for that. Their power is in meaning:

- **Accessibility**: Screen readers say, "Here's the main content" or "This is navigation," helping users skip around.

- **SEO**: Google boosts pages with clear structure—<article> and <main> signal what's worth indexing.

- **Readability**: Your code screams intent—<footer> beats <div class="bottom"> for clarity.

- **Future-Proofing**: HTML5's semantics are the web's current standard—your pages stay relevant.

Try It Out

Open your text editor (Chapter 4) and tweak your "index.html" with these tags. Swap a <p> for an <article>, add a <nav> with links, or wrap content in <section>. Test it in Chrome or Firefox (Chapter 5)—it'll look the same, but check the developer tools (right-click > Inspect). The DOM reflects your semantic structure—cool, right? Add comments (Chapter 10) like <!-- Blog posts start here --> to keep track.

Tips for Semantic Success

- **Don't Overuse**: <header> isn't for every heading—save it for big intros.

- **Match Meaning**: Use <article> for standalone stuff, not random blurbs.

- **Nest Wisely**: <section> can hold <article>, but keep it logical.

- **Test It**: Open your page in a browser—does the structure make sense?

Chapter 12
Headings (\<h1\> to \<h6\>)

You've got semantic tags like \<header\> and \<main\> shaping your page, and now it's time to zoom in on a key player we've used but not fully explored: headings. The \<h1\> to \<h6\> tags are more than just big, bold text—they're the signposts of your webpage, guiding readers and browsers through your content. They create hierarchy, boost readability, and even help search engines figure out what's important. In this chapter, we'll break down how these six tags work, why they matter, and how to use them like a pro. Let's get your page organized, one heading at a time!

What Are Headings?

Headings are HTML tags that mark titles or section breaks, ranging from \<h1\> (the biggest and boldest) to \<h6\> (the smallest). They're like the chapter titles and subheadings in a book—\<h1\> might be "Chapter 1," \<h2\> could be "Section 1.1," and so on. By default, browsers make them stand out (bigger fonts, bolded), but their real power is in structure, not just style. Here's a quick peek:

```
<h1>This is the Main Title</h1>

<h2>A Subsection</h2>

<h3>A Smaller Point</h3>
```

Open that in a browser (Chapter 5), and you'll see the text size shrink from \<h1\> to \<h3\>—instant hierarchy.

The Heading Lineup: \<h1\> to \<h6\>

There are six levels, and each has a job:

- **\<h1\>**: The top dog—usually the page's main title. Use it once per page for the big idea (e.g., "My Blog").

- **\<h2\>**: Major sections under \<h1\>—think "About Me" or "Latest Posts."

- **<h3>**: Subsections within <h2>—like "My Hobbies" under "About Me."

- **<h4> to <h6>**: Deeper levels—rarely needed unless your page is super detailed (e.g., "My Favorite Books" under "Hobbies").

Here's how they fit together:

```html
<!DOCTYPE html>
<html lang="en">
<head>
    <meta charset="UTF-8">
    <title>Heading Demo</title>
</head>
<body>
    <!-- Main page title -->
    <h1>My Website</h1>
    <!-- First big section -->
    <h2>About Me</h2>
    <p>I'm a web learner.</p>
    <!-- Subsection -->
    <h3>My Skills</h3>
    <p>HTML5 and counting!</p>
    <!-- Another big section -->
    <h2>My Blog</h2>
    <p>Thoughts and stuff.</p>
    <h3>Post 1</h3>
    <p>First post here.</p>
</body>
</html>
```

← → C 🔍 index.html   ⊙ ☆ ⋯ 🌼

My Website

About Me

I'm a web learner.

My Skills

HTML5 and counting!

My Blog

Thoughts and stuff.

Post 1

First post here.

Test this in your project folder (Chapter 6)—it's a simple page with a clear outline.

Why Headings Matter

Headings aren't just decoration—they're functional:

1. **Readability**: They break up walls of text, making your page skimmable. Users love that—nobody reads every word online.

2. **Structure**: They build a hierarchy the browser turns into the DOM (Chapter 2). <h1> is the root idea, <h2> branches off, and so on.

3. **SEO**: Search engines like Google weigh headings heavily—<h1> signals "This is what the page is about," boosting your rank if it's clear.

4. **Accessibility**: Screen readers use headings to navigate—users can jump from <h1> to <h2> like a table of contents.

How to Use Them Right

Headings are easy, but a few rules keep them sharp:

- **One <h1> Per Page**: It's the king—don't confuse browsers or search engines with multiples. (Exceptions exist, like in <article> tags, but keep it simple for now.)

- **Don't Skip Levels**: Go <h1> to <h2> to <h3>—jumping from <h1> to <h4> messes up the outline. It's like skipping "Chapter 2" in a book.

- **Content, Not Style**: Use <h1> for importance, not just because you want big text—CSS (coming soon) handles looks.

- **Keep It Short**: <h1>Introduction to My Amazing Website Project</h1> works, but <h1>About Me</h1> is snappier.

Headings in Semantic Context

Pair headings with semantic tags (Chapter 11) for extra power:

```
<header>
    <h1>My Site</h1>
</header>
<main>
    <section>
        <h2>News</h2>
        <article>
            <h3>Post Title</h3>
            <p>Post text.</p>
        </article>
    </section>
</main>
<footer>
    <h2>Contact</h2>
    <p>Email me!</p>
</footer>
```

Here, <h1> crowns the page, <h2> divides major sections, and <h3> flags individual posts—all wrapped in meaningful containers.

Try It Out

Open your "index.html" in your text editor (Chapter 4). Add headings:

- Replace a <p> with <h1>My Page</h1>.

- Add <h2>Section One</h2> and <h3>Subpoint</h3> below it, with <p> text under each.

- Test it in Chrome or Firefox (Chapter 5)—see the size difference? Add a comment (Chapter 10) like <!-- Main heading --> above <h1>.

Tweak it—swap <h2> for <h4>, or add more levels. Open developer tools (right-click > Inspect) and check the "Accessibility" tab—headings build an outline automatically.

Tips for Heading Success

- **Be Descriptive**: <h2>Skills</h2> beats <h2>Stuff</h2>—clarity wins.

- **Test the Flow**: Read headings alone—do they tell a story?

- **Avoid Overkill**: <h6> is rare—stick to <h1>-<h3> for most pages.

- **Preview It**: Refresh your browser after changes—does it *feel* organized?

Why Headings Are Your Ally

Headings turn a blob of text into a roadmap. They're simple to use, baked into HTML5, and universal across browsers. Master them, and your pages don't just look good—they make sense to everyone (and everything) reading them.

Chapter 13
Paragraphs, Line Breaks, and Horizontal Rules

You've got headings sorting your page into neat sections, and now it's time to fill them with text that flows and looks good. Enter three HTML workhorses: <p> for paragraphs, <br> for line breaks, and <hr> for horizontal rules. These tags handle the meat of your content—sentences, spacing, and separators—turning raw text into something readable and organized. They're simple but mighty, and by the end of this chapter, you'll use them to shape your page like a pro. Let's break it down and get your words in line!

The Players: <p>, <br>, and <hr>

These tags are all about text layout—no fancy animations, just the basics done right. Here's a quick teaser:

```
<p>This is a paragraph.</p>

<p>Another one<br>with a line break.</p>

<hr>

<p>Below the line!</p>
```

Test that in your browser (Chapter 5), and you'll see two paragraphs, a mid-sentence break, and a dividing line. Let's unpack each one.

1. <p>: The Paragraph Tag

- **What It Does**: The <p> tag wraps blocks of text—like sentences or short stories—into paragraphs. Browsers add space above and below it by default, making it a natural chunk of content.

Example:

```
<p>Welcome to my site. It's a work in progress.</p>

<p>I hope you like it anyway!</p>
```

- **Why It's Great**: It's the go-to for most text—readable, spaced out, and semantic (it *means* "paragraph"). You've seen it in <main> or <article> (Chapter 11).

- **How It Works**: Open <p>, add text, close </p>. Nest tags like <strong> inside—<p><strong>Bold</strong> text here.</p>—but don't nest <p> inside <p> (that's a no-no).

2.
: The Line Break

- **What It Does**: The <br> tag forces a new line *within* a block of text—like hitting "Enter" in a note. It's self-closing (no </br> needed).

Example:

```
<p>My address:<br>123 Web Lane<br>Codetown, HTML</p>
```

Output:

My address:
123 Web Lane
Codetown, HTML

- **Why It's Great**: Perfect for lists, addresses, or poems—anytime you need a break without starting a new paragraph's spacing.

- **How It Works**: Drop <br> where you want the line to split. Don't overuse it—too many <br> tags can replace proper structure (like <p> or headings).

3. <hr>: The Horizontal Rule

- **What It Does**: The <hr> tag draws a horizontal line across the page—a visual separator. It's self-closing too (no </hr>).

Example:

```
<p>End of intro.</p>

<hr>

<p>Start of main content.</p>
```

Output: A paragraph, a line, then another paragraph.

- **Why It's Great**: It splits sections cleanly—like a divider between topics or a "scene break" in a story. HTML5 treats it semantically as a thematic shift.

- **How It Works**: Plop <hr> between blocks. Browsers style it as a thin gray line (CSS can jazz it up later).

Putting It Together

Here's a full example tying it to semantic tags and headings:

```
<!DOCTYPE html>
<html lang="en">
<head>
    <meta charset="UTF-8">
    <title>Text Demo</title>
    <!-- Link to CSS later -->
    <link rel="stylesheet" href="css/style.css">
</head>
<body>
    <header>
        <h1>My Text Page</h1>
    </header>
    <main>
        <!-- Intro section -->
```

```
            <section>
                <h2>About This Page</h2>
                <p>This is a demo of text tags.<br>It's pretty simple
    so far.</p>
            </section>
            <hr>
            <!-- Details section -->
            <section>
                <h2>More Info</h2>
                <p>I'm learning HTML5.<br>Next up: CSS!</p>
            </section>
        </main>
    </body>
</html>
```

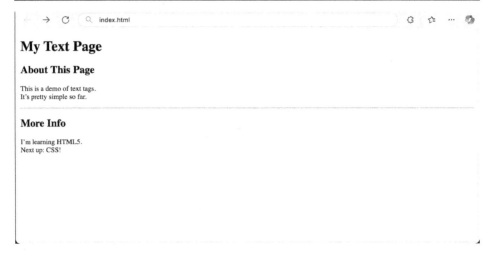

Save this as "index.html" (Chapter 6), open it in Chrome or Firefox, and you'll see a page with a title, two sections separated by a line, and text with breaks. It's basic but structured—perfect for adding more later.

Why These Tags Matter

- **Readability**: <p> chunks text, <br> splits lines, <hr> divides topics—users can skim without drowning in words.

- **Semantics**: They hint at meaning—<p> is content, <hr> is a shift—which helps accessibility tools and search engines.

- **Flexibility**: They're universal across browsers and ready for CSS styling (e.g., making <hr> dotted or <p> colorful).

Try It Out

Open your text editor (Chapter 4) and tweak your "index.html":

- Add <p> tags with a few sentences—maybe a bio or a story.

- Insert <br> mid-paragraph—like a list of favorite foods: <p>My faves:
Pizza
Tacos</p>.

- Drop an <hr> between two <section> tags or after an <h2>.

Test it in your browsers (Chapter 5)—refresh and watch the layout shift. Add comments (Chapter 10) like <!-- Section break --> above <hr> to keep track.

Tips for Text Mastery

- **Use <p> First**: It's your default—only break to <br> or <hr> when needed.

- **Avoid
 Abuse**: Don't stack

 for spacing—<p> or CSS is cleaner.

- **Keep <hr> Purposeful**: It's a divider, not decor—tie it to a content shift.

- **Check Flow**: Read your page—does it *feel* easy to follow?

Chapter 14
Lists: Ordered, Unordered, and Description Lists

You've got paragraphs and headings shaping your page, and now it's time to tackle another content champ: lists. Whether you're ranking your top movies, bulleting your skills, or defining terms, HTML5's list tags—<ol> for ordered, <ul> for unordered, and <dl> for descriptions—have you covered. These tags turn jumbled ideas into neat, scannable groups, making your page easier to read and more professional. By the end of this chapter, you'll wield lists like a pro, adding order and clarity to your <main> section. Let's list it up!

Why Lists Matter

Lists are everywhere—think menus, to-dos, or ingredients. On the web, they break up text (Chapter 13), highlight key points, and guide the eye. They're semantic too—browsers, search engines, and screen readers understand them as structured data, not just decoration. HTML5 gives you three flavors to match your needs: numbered, bulleted, or term-definition pairs. Here's the rundown.

1. <ol>: Ordered Lists

- **What It Does**: The <ol> tag (ordered list) creates a numbered list—perfect for steps, rankings, or anything with a sequence. Each item goes in an <li> (list item) tag.

Example:

```
<ol>
    <li>Wake up</li>
    <li>Learn HTML</li>
    <li>Build a site</li>
</ol>
```

Output:

- **Why It's Great**: Numbers show priority or order—great for tutorials or top-10s.

- **How It Works**: Wrap <li> tags in <ol> and <ol>—the browser adds numbers automatically.

2. <ul>: Unordered Lists

- **What It Does**: The <ul> tag (unordered list) makes a bulleted list—ideal for items without a specific order, like features or groceries. Uses <li> too.

Example:

```
<ul>

    <li>Coffee</li>

    <li>Code</li>

    <li>Repeat</li>

</ul>
```

- **Why It's Great**: Bullets keep it simple—perfect for quick, equal-weight points.

- **How It Works**: Same as <ol>, but <ul> swaps numbers for bullets (dots by default—CSS can tweak this later).

- Coffee
- Code
- Repeat

3. <dl>: Description Lists

- **What It Does**: The <dl> tag (description list) pairs terms with details—think dictionaries or FAQs. It uses <dt> (description term) and <dd> (description definition).

Example:

```
<dl>

    <dt>HTML</dt>

    <dd>HyperText Markup Language</dd>

    <dt>CSS</dt>

    <dd>Cascading Style Sheets</dd>

</dl>
```

- **Why It's Great**: It's semantic for key-value pairs—browsers indent <dd> under <dt> for clarity.

- **How It Works**: Wrap <dt> and <dd> in <dl>—one <dt> can have multiple <dd>s (e.g., a term with two meanings).

Lists in Action

Here's a full page mixing all three with semantic tags (Chapter 11):

```
<!DOCTYPE html>
<html lang="en">
<head>
    <meta charset="UTF-8">
    <title>List Demo</title>
    <!-- Add CSS later -->
    <link rel="stylesheet" href="css/style.css">
</head>
<body>
    <header>
        <h1>My List Page</h1>
    </header>
    <main>
        <!-- Steps to learn -->
        <section>
            <h2>How I'm Learning</h2>
            <ol>
                <li>Read this book</li>
                <li>Practice tags</li>
                <li>Build something cool</li>
            </ol>
        </section>
        <!-- My skills -->
        <section>
            <h2>Skills So Far</h2>
            <ul>
                <li>HTML5</li>
                <li>Headings</li>
                <li>Lists</li>
            </ul>
        </section>
        <!-- Terms I know -->
```

```
        <section>
            <h2>Web Terms</h2>
            <dl>
                <dt>Tag</dt>
                <dd>A markup instruction</dd>
                <dt>Browser</dt>
                <dd>Renders my code</dd>
            </dl>
        </section>
    </main>
</body>
</html>
```

Save this as "index.html" (Chapter 6), test it in your browsers (Chapter 5), and you'll see a page with a numbered plan, bulleted skills, and defined terms—all tidy and purposeful.

Why These Tags Shine

- **Clarity**: Lists make info digestible—users skim them faster than paragraphs.

- **Semantics**: <ol> means order, <ul> means items, <dl> means definitions—better than plain <p> for structured data.

- **Flexibility**: Nest them (e.g., <ul> inside <li>) or style them with CSS later for custom looks.

Try It Out

Open your text editor (Chapter 4) and tweak your "index.html":

- Add an <ol> with three steps—like a recipe or plan.

- Toss in a <ul> with four favorites—movies, foods, whatever.

- Create a <dl> with two terms and meanings—like web jargon or pet names.

Add comments (Chapter 10) like <!-- My to-do list --> above <ol>. Test it in Chrome or Firefox—refresh and admire the order. Play—swap <ol> for <ul> and see the difference.

Tips for List Success

- **Keep Items Short**: <li>Pizza</li> beats a paragraph—lists are snappy.

- **Match the Type**: Use <ol> for order, <ul> for chaos, <dl> for pairs.

- **Nest Carefully**: <ul><li>Item<ul><li>Subitem</li></ul></li></ul> works—test it!

- **Don't Force It**: If it's one sentence, use <p>—lists need multiple items.

Chapter 15
Creating Hyperlinks (<a>)

You've got text flowing with paragraphs, lists organizing your ideas, and headings guiding the way. Now it's time to add the web's superpower: hyperlinks. The <a> tag (short for "anchor") turns words or images into clickable portals, linking your page to other pages, sites, or even spots within the same document. It's what makes the web *hyper*—a network of connections you can navigate with a tap. By the end of this chapter, you'll weave links into your HTML5 pages like a digital trailblazer. Let's anchor in and get clicking!

What's a Hyperlink?

A hyperlink is a clickable piece of content—usually text—that takes you somewhere else when you tap it. The <a> tag makes it happen, and its href attribute (hypertext reference) tells the browser where to go. Think of it as a door: <a> is the frame, href is the address, and the text inside is the sign saying "Enter Here." Here's a taste:

```
<a href="https://example.com">Visit Example</a>
```

In your browser (Chapter 5), "Visit Example" turns blue and clickable— click it, and you're off to example.com.

The <a> Tag Basics

- **What It Does**: Wraps content (text, images) and links it to a destination.

- **Key Attribute**: href—the URL or path to the target.

Example:

```
<p>Check out <a href="https://google.com">Google</a> for more info.</p>
```

Output: "Google" becomes a link in your paragraph.

Types of Links

The <a> tag is versatile—here's how it connects different destinations:

1. External Links

- **What**: Links to other websites.

How:

```
<a href="https://wikipedia.org">Learn Stuff</a>
```

- **Tip**: Use full URLs (with "https://") for sites outside your project.

2. Internal Links

- **What**: Links to other pages in your project (Chapter 6's folder structure).

How:

```
<a href="about.html">About Me</a>
```

- **Tip**: Use relative paths—like "about.html" if it's in the same folder, or "pages/about.html" if it's in a subfolder.

3. Anchor Links

- **What**: Links to a spot on the same page—great for long content.

How:

```
<a href="#bottom">Jump to Bottom</a>
<!-- Lots of content... -->
<h2 id="bottom">The Bottom</h2>
```

- **Tip**: Add an id attribute to the target, then link with #id-name.

Links in Action

Here's a full page with all three types:

```html
<!DOCTYPE html>
<html lang="en">
<head>
    <meta charset="UTF-8">
    <title>Link Demo</title>
    <!-- CSS link -->
    <link rel="stylesheet" href="css/style.css">
</head>
<body>
    <header>
        <h1>My Linked Site</h1>
        <!-- Navigation with internal links -->
        <nav>
            <a href="index.html">Home</a> |
            <a href="about.html">About</a>
        </nav>
    </header>
    <main>
        <section>
            <h2>Explore</h2>
            <p>Visit <a href="https://x.com">X</a> for updates.</p>
            <p>Or <a href="#info">jump below</a> for more.</p>
        </section>
        <!-- Spacer for demo -->
        <p>(Imagine lots of text here...)</p>
        <hr>
        <section id="info">
            <h2>More Info</h2>
            <p>You made it! Back to <a href="#top">top</a>.</p>
```

```
        </section>
    </main>
</body>
</html>
```

Save this as "index.html" (Chapter 6), test it in your browser, and click around—external to X, internal (make an "about.html" stub if you want), and anchor links to jump.

Extra <a> Tricks

- **Open in New Tab**: Add target="_blank":

```
<a href="https://github.com" target="_blank">GitHub</a>
```

Keeps your page open—handy for external links.

- **Link Images**: Wrap <img> in <a>:

```
<a href="https://example.com"><img src="images/logo.jpg" al-
t="Logo"></a>
```

Click the image, go somewhere—cool, right?

- **Email Links**: Use mailto::

```
<a href="mailto:me@example.com">Email Me</a>
```

Opens the user's email app.

Why Links Rule

- **Connectivity**: They tie your site to the web—or itself—making it interactive.

- **Navigation**: <nav> (Chapter 11) with <a> tags builds menus users love.

- **Semantics**: <a> tells assistive tech "This is a link," boosting accessibility.

- **Engagement**: Links invite exploration—key to keeping visitors around.

Try It Out

Open your text editor (Chapter 4) and tweak your "index.html":

- Add an external link—<a href="https://yourfavesite.com">My Fave</a>.

- Create an internal link—<a href="contact.html">Contact</a> (make a blank "contact.html" to test).

- Set an anchor—add <h2 id="end">End</h2> and link to it with <a href="#end">Go to End</a>.

Add comments (Chapter 10) like <!-- External link -->. Test in Chrome or Firefox (Chapter 5)—click and explore. Break it—use a bad URL, fix it, learn!

Tips for Link Success

- **Be Descriptive**: <a href="#">Click here</a> is vague—<a href="#">Read More</a> is better.

- **Check Paths**: "about.html" won't work if it's not in your folder (Chapter 6).

- **Test Every Link**: Click them all—404 errors are no fun.

- **Style Later**: Links are blue and underlined now—CSS will fix that soon.

Chapter 16
Linking to External Pages, Internal Sections, and Emails

Last chapter, you unlocked the <a> tag and started connecting your pages to the world. Now, let's fine-tune that skill by mastering three key linking moves: pointing to external websites, jumping to sections within your page, and triggering email actions. The <a> tag's href attribute is your wand here, and with a few tricks, you'll turn your site into a hub of navigation—inside, outside, and beyond. By the end, you'll link like a seasoned web weaver, making your pages both useful and interactive. Let's hop to it!

The Power of href

The <a> tag's magic lies in its href attribute—it's the address telling the browser where to go. Last time, we touched on external, internal, and email links; now we'll dig into each, with examples you can test. All links start the same: <a href="destination">Click Me</a>—it's the "destination" that changes the game.

1. Linking to External Pages

- **What It Does**: Sends users to another website—anywhere on the web.

How:

```
<p>Learn more at <a href="https://www.raphaelheide.com">
Raphael Heide</a>.</p>
```

Output: "Raphael Heide" links to their site.

- **Key Details**: Use the full URL—https:// included—to reach outside your project (Chapter 6's folder). Add target="_blank" to open it in a new tab:

```
<a href="https://developer.mozilla.org" target="_blank">MDN
Docs</a>
```

- **Why It's Useful**: Connects your site to resources, references, or socials—think "Follow me on X" or "Read this article."

2. Linking to Internal Sections

- **What It Does**: Jumps to a spot on the same page—perfect for long content or quick navigation.

How:

```
<!-- Top of page -->

<p><a href="#skills">See my skills</a></p>

<!-- Later in page -->

<section id="skills">

    <h2>My Skills</h2>

    <p>HTML5 and more!</p>

</section>
```

Output: Click "See my skills," and you zip to the <section>.

- **Key Details**: Use # plus an id (like #skills) to target an element with that id attribute. Add a "Back to top" link:

```
<a href="#top">Back to top</a>
```

(Tag <body id="top"> or another high element.)

- **Why It's Useful**: Saves scrolling—great for FAQs, tables of contents, or blog posts with subheads (Chapter 12).

3. Linking to Emails

- **What It Does**: Opens the user's email app with a pre-filled "To" field—handy for "Contact me" links.

How:

```
<p>Reach me at

<a href="mailto:you@example.com">you@example.com</a>.</p>
```

Output: Click it, and your email client pops up.

- **Key Details**: Use mailto: followed by the address. Fancy it up with a subject:

```
<a href="mailto:you@example.com?subject=Hello">Email Me</a>
```

- **Why It's Useful**: Makes contacting you a breeze—no copying and pasting needed.

A Full Example

Here's a page mixing all three, with semantic tags (Chapter 11):

```
<!DOCTYPE html>
<html lang="en">
<head>
    <meta charset="UTF-8">
    <title>Link Types</title>
    <!-- CSS link -->
    <link rel="stylesheet" href="css/style.css">
</head>
<body id="top">
    <header>
        <h1>My Site</h1>
        <!-- Internal nav -->
        <nav>
            <a href="#bio">Bio</a> |
            <a href="mailto:me@example.com">Contact</a>
```

```
            </nav>

        </header>

        <main>

            <section>

                <h2>Welcome</h2>

                <p>Check out <a href="https://html5.org" target="_
blank">HTML5.org</a>!</p>

                <p>Or jump to my <a href="#bio">bio below</a>.</p>

            </section>

            <!-- Spacer for demo -->

            <p>(Lots of text here...)</p>

            <hr>

            <section id="bio">

                <h2>Bio</h2>

                <p>I'm learning web dev. <a href="#top">Back to top</
a>.</p>

            </section>

        </main>

    </body>

</html>
```

My Site

Bio ❘ Contact

Welcome

Check out HTML5.org!

Or jump to my bio below.

(Lots of text here...)

Bio

I'm learning web dev. Back to top.

Save this as "index.html" (Chapter 6), test it in your browser (Chapter 5), and click around—external site in a new tab, email app popping up, and smooth jumps within the page.

Why These Links Rock

- **External**: Ties your site to the web—credibility and resources at a click.

- **Internal**: Keeps users engaged without leaving—navigation made simple.

- **Email**: Turns "Contact me" into action—direct and personal.

- **Semantics**: <a> with clear href values boosts accessibility—screen readers announce destinations.

Try It Out

Open your text editor (Chapter 4) and tweak your "index.html":

- Add an external link—<a href="https://yourfavesite.com" target="_blank">My Fave</a>.

- Create an internal jump—add <h2 id="end">End</h2> and <a href="#end">Go There</a>.

- Toss in an email link—<a href="mailto:you@example.com">E-mail Me</a>.

Add comments (Chapter 10) like <!-- External resource -->. Test in Chrome or Firefox—click each link. Break it—use a fake URL, fix it, learn!

Tips for Linking Success

- **Full URLs for External**: "https://x.com" works; "x.com" might not.

- **Unique IDs**: #bio can't link to two spots—keep id values one-of-a-kind.

- **Test Every Click**: External links 404? Internal jumps miss? Check your href.

- **Clear Text**: <a href="#">Email</a> beats <a href="#">Click here</a>—say where it goes.

Chapter 17
Adding Images (<img>)
and Optimizing Them for the Web

You've got links connecting your pages to the world, and now it's time to make them pop with visuals. The <img> tag is your ticket to adding images—photos, logos, or memes—to your HTML5 site, turning plain text into something eye-catching. But it's not just about slapping pictures in; you'll also need to optimize them so your pages load fast and look great everywhere. By the end of this chapter, you'll master the <img> tag and some web-friendly tricks to keep your site snappy. Let's paint the web with pixels!

The <img> Tag: Bringing in the Visuals

- **What It Does**: The <img> tag embeds an image into your page—no closing tag needed (it's self-closing).

- **Key Attributes**:

  o src: The image's file path or URL (like "images/cat.jpg").

  o alt: Text describing the image—for accessibility and if it fails to load.

- **Example**:

```
<img src="images/dog.jpg" alt="A fluffy dog">
```

Output: A dog pic appears where you put the tag (assuming "dog.jpg" is in your "images" folder from Chapter 6).

Adding Images to Your Page

Here's a simple page with an image:

```
<!DOCTYPE html>
<html lang="en">
<head>
    <meta charset="UTF-8">
    <title>Image Demo</title>
    <!-- CSS link -->
    <link rel="stylesheet" href="css/style.css">
</head>
<body>
    <header>
        <h1>My Site</h1>
    </header>
    <main>
        <section>
            <h2>My Pet</h2>
            <p>Meet my buddy:</p>
            <!-- My dog photo -->
            <img src="images/dog.jpg" alt="My dog smiling">
        </section>
    </main>
</body>
</html>
```

My Site

My Pet

Meet my buddy:

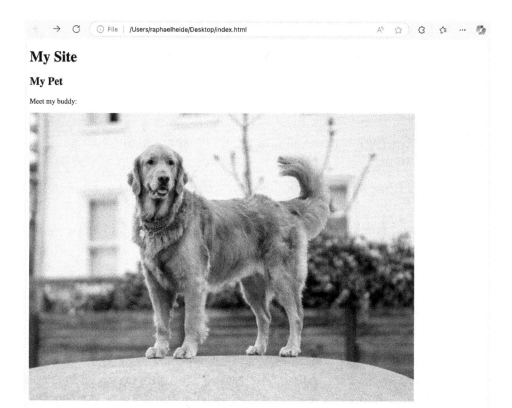

Save this as "index.html" (Chapter 6), grab a photo (rename it "dog.jpg"), drop it in your "images" folder, and test it in your browser (Chapter 5). Boom—visuals!

Linking Images

Combine <img> with <a> (Chapter 15) for clickable pics:

```
<a href="https://example.com">

    <img src="images/logo.jpg" alt="Site logo">

</a>
```

Click the logo, and you're off—great for banners or portfolios.

Optimizing Images for the Web

Images are awesome, but big files slow your site down—users hate waiting, and search engines ding you for it. Here's how to keep them web-ready:

1. Pick the Right Format

- **JPEG (.jpg)**: Best for photos—good quality, small size. Use it for "dog.jpg."

- **PNG (.png)**: Great for logos or graphics with transparency—sharp edges, but bigger files.

- **GIF (.gif)**: Simple animations or tiny icons—limited colors, avoid for photos.

2. Shrink the File Size

- **Resize**: Crop or scale images to the size you'll display (e.g., 500px wide, not 5000px). Use tools like Paint, Preview, or online editors (try tinypng.com).

- **Compress**: Reduce quality slightly—80% JPEG quality looks fine but cuts size. Free tools like GIMP or Photoshop work, or use web-based options.

3. Name Smartly

- Use lowercase, no spaces—dog-photo.jpg, not "Dog Photo.jpg"—web servers love it (Chapter 6).

4. Use alt Wisely

- **Why**: Screen readers read alt for blind users; it shows if the image breaks.

- **How**: <img src="images/cat.jpg" alt="Black cat on a mat">—specific, not "image" or blank.

A Real-World Example

Here's an optimized setup:

```
<!DOCTYPE html>

<html lang="en">

<head>

    <meta charset="UTF-8">
```

```html
        <title>Optimized Images</title>
    </head>
    <body>
        <header>
            <h1>My Gallery</h1>
            <!-- Navigation -->
            <nav>
                <a href="#pics">See Pics</a>
            </nav>
        </header>
        <main>
            <section id="pics">
                <h2>My Photos</h2>
                <!-- Optimized JPEG, 500px wide -->
                <img src="images/beach.jpg" alt="Sunset at the beach">
                <p>A sunset I caught last week.</p>
                <!-- Linked PNG logo -->
                <a href="https://myblog.com">
                    <img src="images/logo.png" alt="My blog logo">
                </a>
            </section>
        </main>
    </body>
</html>
```

Prep two images: a compressed "beach.jpg" (JPEG, ~500px wide) and a small "logo.png" (PNG with transparency). Test it—fast and sharp!

Why Images and Optimization Matter

- **Engagement**: Pics grab attention—text alone can't compete.

- **Accessibility**: alt text ensures everyone "sees" your images.

- **Performance**: Optimized files mean quick loads—key for mobile users (half the web's traffic).

- **Professionalism**: Clean, fast images scream "I know what I'm doing."

Try It Out

Open your text editor (Chapter 4) and tweak your "index.html":

- Add an <img>—grab a photo, save it as "pic.jpg" in "images/," and use <img src="images/pic.jpg" alt="My pic">.

- Link it—wrap it in <a href="https://example.com">.

- Optimize—resize it to 600px wide, compress it online, and retest.

Add comments (Chapter 10) like <!-- Hero image -->. Test in Chrome or Firefox (Chapter 5)—check load time (developer tools > Network tab). Too slow? Shrink it more!

Tips for Image Success

- **Path Check**: "images/pic.jpg" fails if it's not there—double-check your folder (Chapter 6).

- **Alt Always**: <img src="x.jpg" alt=""> is lazy—describe it.

- **Test Sizes**: Open on your phone—does it fit? Too big? Adjust.

- **Backup Originals**: Edit copies—keep raw files safe.

Chapter 18
Using Figure and Figcaption

You've got images popping onto your pages with <img>, and now it's time to give them some context and class. Enter HTML5's <figure> and <figcaption> tags—a dynamic duo for wrapping visuals (like photos, diagrams, or charts) with captions that explain what's going on. These semantic tags don't just decorate; they tell the browser, search engines, and screen readers that this image and its caption belong together. By the end of this chapter, you'll use <figure> and <figcaption> to make your visuals smarter and your pages more professional. Let's frame it up!

What Are <figure> and <figcaption>?

- **<figure>**: A container for self-contained content—think images, illustrations, or code snippets—that's related to your main text but can stand alone or be moved without breaking the flow.

- **<figcaption>**: A caption or description for the <figure>'s content, nestled inside it. It's optional but adds meaning.

Together, they're like a museum exhibit: <figure> is the frame, <figcaption> is the plaque. Here's a quick look:

```
<figure>
    <img src="images/cat.jpg" alt="A cat napping">
    <figcaption>A sleepy kitty enjoying the sun.</figcaption>
</figure>
```

Test this in your browser (Chapter 5)—the image shows up with a caption below, neatly tied together.

Why Use Them?

These tags aren't just <img> with extra steps—they're semantic superheroes:

- **Clarity**: <figcaption> explains the image—users know why it's there.

- **Semantics**: <figure> flags the content as a unit—browsers and assistive tech treat it as one piece, not scattered parts.

- **SEO**: Search engines love captioned images—more context, better indexing.

- **Flexibility**: Move a <figure> elsewhere (like a sidebar), and it still makes sense.

How They Work

- **Structure**: Wrap <img> (or other content) and <figcaption> in <figure>. The caption can go before or after—usually after for images.

Example:

```
<p>Cats are great pets.</p>

<figure>

    <img src="images/cat.jpg" alt="Cat on a windowsill">

    <figcaption>My cat basking in the morning light.</figcaption>

</figure>

<p>They love to nap!</p>
```

Output: Text, then an image with a caption, then more text—clean and connected.

Beyond Images

<figure> isn't just for <img>—try it with code, quotes, or diagrams:

```
<figure>

    <pre><code>&lt;p&gt;Hello, world!&lt;/p&gt;</code></pre>

    <figcaption>Example of a basic HTML paragraph.</figcaption>

</figure>
```

Here, <pre> and <code> (more on those later) show code, captioned for context.

A Full Page Example

Here's a page with <figure> in action, tied to semantic tags (Chapter 11):

```
<!DOCTYPE html>
<html lang="en">
<head>
    <meta charset="UTF-8">
    <title>Figure Demo</title>
    <!-- CSS link -->
    <link rel="stylesheet" href="css/style.css">
</head>
<body>
    <header>
        <h1>My Photo Journal</h1>
        <nav>
            <a href="#pics">Photos</a>
        </nav>
    </header>
    <main>
        <section id="pics">
            <h2>My Adventures</h2>
            <p>I love capturing moments.</p>
            <!-- First figure -->
            <figure>
                <img src="images/beach.jpg" alt="Beach at sun-
set">
                <figcaption>Sunset over the coast, March 2025.</
figcaption>
            </figure>
            <!-- Second figure -->
            <figure>
                <img src="images/mountain.jpg" alt="Mountain
```

```
hike">
                    <figcaption>Climbing up high last weekend.</figcap-
tion>
                </figure>
            </section>
        </main>
    </body>
</html>
```

Save this as "index.html" (Chapter 6), add "beach.jpg" and "mountain.
jpg" to your "images" folder (optimized per Chapter 17), and test it. You'll
see a journal with captioned photos—structured and story-driven.

My Photo Journal

Photos

My Adventures

I love capturing moments.

Sunset over the coast, March 2025.

Climbing up high last weekend.

Pairing with Links

Make figures clickable (Chapter 15):

```
<figure>
    <a href="https://mygallery.com">
        <img src="images/art.jpg" alt="Abstract painting">
    </a>
    <figcaption>My latest artwork—click to see more.</figcaption>
```

```
</figure>
```

Click the image, not the caption—perfect for portfolios.

Why They Matter

- **Accessibility**: Screen readers say, "Figure with caption," then read the alt and <figcaption>—users get the full picture.

- **Organization**: <figure> groups visuals logically—better than loose <img> tags.

- **Style Ready**: CSS (coming soon) can target <figure> and <figcaption> for custom layouts or borders.

Try It Out

Open your text editor (Chapter 4) and tweak your "index.html":

- Add a <figure> with an <img>—use a photo from "images/" and an alt.

- Write a <figcaption>—describe the image in a sentence.

- Test a linked figure—wrap <img> in <a href="https://example. com">.

Add comments (Chapter 10) like <!-- Photo with caption -->. Test in Chrome or Firefox (Chapter 5)—refresh and check developer tools (Accessibility tab) to see the semantic grouping.

Tips for Figure Success

- **Match Content**: Use <figure> for standalone visuals—random decor pics might just need <img>.

- **Short Captions**: <figcaption>A sunny day</figcaption> beats an essay.

- **Alt vs. Caption**: alt describes for accessibility; <figcaption> adds context—don't repeat verbatim.

- **Test Flow**: Move the <figure>—does the page still make sense?

Chapter 19
Setting Image Dimensions
(Width and Height)

You've got images lighting up your pages with <img> and <figure>, and now it's time to take control of how they look. The width and height attributes for the <img> tag let you set exact dimensions, ensuring your visuals fit perfectly—whether it's a tiny logo or a sprawling banner. But it's not just about looks; sizing images right keeps your page fast and user-friendly. By the end of this chapter, you'll wield width and height like a design wizard, making your site sharp and snappy. Let's size things up!

Why Set Image Dimensions?

Images without dimensions can be wildcards—browsers guess their size, which might stretch them weirdly or slow your page as it adjusts. Adding width and height:

- Locks in the space upfront—text won't jump around while images load.

- Scales visuals to fit your layout—no awkward cropping or overflow.

- Ties into optimization (Chapter 17)—matching display size to file size saves bandwidth.

The width and height Attributes

- **What They Do**: Tell the browser how wide and tall an image should be, in pixels (px) or sometimes percentages (%).

- **How They Work**: Add them to <img>—no CSS needed yet.

Example:

```
<img src="images/cat.jpg" alt="A cat" width="300"
height="200">
```

Output: The cat pic displays at 300px wide and 200px tall, no matter its original size.

Pixels vs. Original Size

- **Original**: If "cat.jpg" is 600x400px, width="300" height="200" shrinks it to half.

- **Mismatch**: Set width="300" height="300", and it distorts—squashing or stretching. Match the aspect ratio (e.g., 600:400 = 3:2) for clean scaling.

Using Them in Practice

Here's a page with sized images:

```
<!DOCTYPE html>
<html lang="en">
<head>
    <meta charset="UTF-8">
    <title>Image Sizes</title>
    <!-- CSS link -->
    <link rel="stylesheet" href="css/style.css">
</head>
<body>
    <header>
        <h1>My Gallery</h1>
    </header>
    <main>
        <section>
            <h2>Small and Big</h2>
            <!-- Thumbnail -->
            <figure>
                <img src="images/beach.jpg" alt="Beach"
width="150" height="100">
                <figcaption>Tiny beach view</figcaption>
            </figure>
            <!-- Full-width -->
```

```
          <figure>

                <img src="images/mountain.jpg" alt="Mountain"
width="600" height="400">

                <figcaption>A grand peak</figcaption>

          </figure>

       </section>

    </main>

</body>

</html>
```

Save this as "index.html" (Chapter 6), use optimized "beach.jpg" and
"mountain.jpg" from your "images" folder (Chapter 17), and test it in your
browser (Chapter 5). You'll see a small thumbnail and a larger shot—sized
just right.

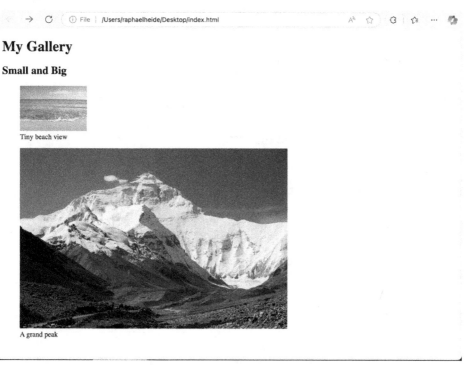

Pair with <a> (Chapter 15):

```
<a href="https://mygallery.com">

    <img src="images/logo.jpg" alt="Logo" width="100"
height="100">

</a>
```

A tidy, clickable 100x100px logo—perfect for navigation.

Optimizing with Dimensions

Setting width and height isn't just display—it's performance:

- **Match File Size**: If you show "beach.jpg" at 150x100px, resize the file to 150x100px (Chapter 17)—don't force the browser to down-scale a 2000x2000px original.

- **Prevent Layout Shift**: Without dimensions, text moves as images load—annoying for users. Set them, and the space is reserved.

- **Test on Mobile**: A 600px-wide image might overflow on a phone—check it (Chapter 5) and adjust.

Pro Tip: Aspect Ratio

To avoid distortion, calculate the ratio:

- Original: 600x400px = 3:2.

- Want 300px wide? Height = 300 × (2 ÷ 3) = 200px.

- Use width="300" height="200"—no squashing!

Why Dimensions Matter

- **Control**: You decide the layout—not the image's raw size.

- **Speed**: Pre-sized slots mean faster rendering (Chapter 2's rendering process).

- **User Experience**: No shifting or stretching—pages look polished.

- **Accessibility**: Screen readers don't care, but alt plus dimensions paint a clearer picture.

Try It Out

Open your text editor (Chapter 4) and tweak your "index.html":

- Add an <img>—<img src="images/pic.jpg" alt="My pic" width="200" height="150">.

- Test distortion—set height="300", see it stretch, then fix it to match the ratio.

- Wrap it in <figure> (Chapter 18) with a <figcaption>.

Add comments (Chapter 10) like <!-- Sized hero image -->. Test in Chrome or Firefox—use developer tools (Network tab) to check load time. Too big? Resize the file!

Tips for Dimension Success

- **Check Originals**: Open your image in a viewer—what's its native size?

- **Stay Proportional**: Mismatched width and height = goofy results.

- **Smaller is Faster**: Don't display 100px but serve a 1000px file—optimize!

- **Preview Everywhere**: Test on desktop and phone—does it fit?

Chapter 20
Using Responsive Images
(srcset and sizes)

You've got images sized with width and height, but the web's a wild place—screens range from tiny phones to giant monitors, and users expect your site to look good everywhere. Enter responsive images with srcset and sizes—HTML5 tools that let the browser pick the best image for the job, based on screen size or resolution. It's like giving your site a wardrobe of outfits, ready for any occasion. By the end of this chapter, you'll make your <img> tags smart and flexible, keeping your pages fast and sharp. Let's get responsive!

Why Responsive Images?

A single <img src="big.jpg"> works, but it's clunky:

- On a phone, a 2000px-wide image wastes data—slow loads, unhappy users.

- On a 4K screen, a 500px image looks blurry—lost detail, amateur vibes.

- Fixed width and height (Chapter 19) help layout, but don't adapt the file itself.

srcset and sizes fix this by offering options—multiple image files—and letting the browser choose, based on device width or pixel density (e.g., Retina screens). It's optimization (Chapter 17) on steroids.

The Tools: srcset and sizes

- srcset: Lists image files with their widths or densities—e.g., "small.jpg 500w, big.jpg 1000w."

- sizes: Hints at how wide the image will display—e.g., "100vw" (full viewport width) or "50vw" (half).

- **Fallback**: The src attribute covers old browsers that don't get srcset.

Here's a basic shot:

```
<img src="images/cat-low.jpg"
     srcset="images/cat-low.jpg 500w, images/cat-high.jpg 1000w"
     sizes="100vw"
     alt="A cat lounging">
```

- src: Default image (500px wide here).

- srcset: Two options—500px or 1000px wide.

- sizes: Displays full-width—browser picks the best file.

How It Works

1. **Prepare Images**: Create versions of "cat.jpg"—e.g., 500px wide ("cat-low.jpg") and 1000px wide ("cat-high.jpg")—optimized (Chapter 17).

2. **List in srcset**: "filename widthw" tells the browser each file's native width.

3. **Set sizes**: Describes the display width—100vw means "full screen width."

4. **Browser Decides**: A 320px phone grabs "cat-low.jpg"; a 1200px desktop takes "cat-high.jpg."

Pixel Density Bonus

For high-res screens (e.g., Retina), use density (x):

```
<img src="images/cat.jpg"
     srcset="images/cat.jpg 1x, images/cat-2x.jpg 2x"
     alt="A sharp cat">
```

- 1x: Standard screens.

- 2x: Double-density (e.g., 1000px file for a 500px slot)—crisp, not blurry.

A Real-World Example

Here's a responsive page:

```html
<!DOCTYPE html>
<html lang="en">
<head>
    <meta charset="UTF-8">
    <title>Responsive Images</title>
    <!-- CSS link -->
    <link rel="stylesheet" href="css/style.css">
</head>
<body>
    <header>
        <h1>My Photo Site</h1>
    </header>
    <main>
        <section>
            <h2>My Trip</h2>
            <figure>
                <!-- Responsive image -->
                <img src="images/beach-low.jpg"
                    srcset="images/beach-low.jpg 500w, images/
beach-med.jpg 1000w, images/beach-high.jpg 2000w"
                    sizes="80vw"
                    alt="Beach sunset">
                <figcaption>Sunset vibes, resized for your
screen.</figcaption>
            </figure>
            <p>Caught this last summer.</p>
        </section>
    </main>
</body>
</html>
```

Save this as "index.html" (Chapter 6), prep three "beach" images (500px, 1000px, 2000px wide), and test it in your browser (Chapter 5). Resize the window or check on your phone—different files load based on width!

Fine-Tuning with sizes

For layouts where images aren't full-width:

```
<img src="images/dog-low.jpg"

    srcset="images/dog-low.jpg 300w, images/dog-high.jpg 600w"

    sizes="(max-width: 600px) 100vw, 50vw"

    alt="A dog">
```

- (max-width: 600px) 100vw: On screens up to 600px, image is full-width.

- 50vw: On wider screens, it's half-width (e.g., a two-column layout).

- Browser picks "dog-low.jpg" or "dog-high.jpg" to match.

Why Responsive Images Win

- **Speed**: Smaller files for smaller screens—less data, faster loads.

- **Quality**: Sharp images on big or high-res screens—no pixelation.

- **User Experience**: Adapts to phones, tablets, laptops—everyone's happy.

- **Future-Proof**: HTML5's srcset is modern web standard—ready for tomorrow.

Try It Out

Open your text editor (Chapter 4) and tweak your "index.html":

- Grab one image (e.g., "pic.jpg"), make two versions—300px and 600px wide.

- Add: <img src="images/pic-low.jpg" srcset="images/pic-low.jpg 300w, images/pic-high.jpg 600w" sizes="100vw" alt="My pic">.

- Test in Chrome or Firefox—resize the window, use developer tools (Network tab) to see which file loads.

Add comments (Chapter 10) like <!-- Responsive hero -->. Check on your phone—does it swap files?

Tips for Responsive Success

- **Multiple Sizes**: Offer 2-4 options—e.g., 400w, 800w, 1600w—cover the range.

- **Match Layout**: Use sizes to reflect your design—test with CSS later.

- **Fallback**: src ensures old browsers (rare now) still work.

- **Inspect It**: Developer tools show which image loads—tweak if it's off.

Chapter 21

Compressing Images for Faster Loading

You've got images sized, responsive, and ready to shine, but there's a catch—big files can drag your site down, leaving users tapping their feet or bouncing away. Compressing images is the fix: shrinking their file size without trashing quality, so your pages load fast and smooth. It's a key piece of web optimization (touched on in Chapter 17), and with tools and tricks, it's easier than you think. By the end of this chapter, you'll slash load times and keep your visuals crisp—making your HTML5 site a speed demon. Let's lighten the load!

Why Compress Images?

Uncompressed images are heavy—think megabytes instead of kilobytes:

- A 5MB photo on a phone (half the web's traffic) chokes slow connections.

- Search engines like Google favor fast sites—slow loads hurt your rank.

- Users expect instant—3 seconds too long, and they're gone.

Compression cuts file size—sometimes by 80%—while keeping what the eye sees. Pair it with width/height (Chapter 19) and srcset (Chapter 20), and your site flies.

How Compression Works

Compression comes in two flavors:

- **Lossy**: Ditches some data (e.g., fine color details)—smaller files, slight quality drop. JPEGs love this.

- **Lossless**: Shrinks without losing a pixel—less dramatic savings, perfect for PNGs or GIFs.

You'll tweak quality (e.g., 80% vs. 100%) or strip extras (like metadata) to hit the sweet spot—small but sharp.

Tools to Get It Done

No coding needed—just software or websites:

1. **Free Online Tools**:

   o **TinyPNG/TinyJPG** (tinypng.com): Drag-and-drop JPEGs or PNGs—cuts size big-time, keeps quality.

   o **Squoosh** (squoosh.app): Adjust compression live, see results, save as JPEG or WebP (a modern format).

2. **Desktop Apps**:

   o **GIMP**: Free, open-source—export with custom quality (e.g., 75%).

   o **Photoshop**: Pro-level—save for web, tweak settings.

3. **Built-In**:

   o **Preview (Mac)**: Export, lower quality slider.

   o **Paint (Windows)**: Resize, save as JPEG.

Step-by-Step Compression

Here's how to compress "beach.jpg":

1. **Start Big**: Say it's 2000x1333px, 2MB—too hefty.

2. **Resize**: Scale to 1000x667px (for width="1000"—Chapter 19) in Paint or TinyPNG.

3. **Compress**: Use TinyJPG, set quality to 80%—drops to ~200KB.

4. **Save**: Name it "beach-med.jpg" (Chapter 6's naming rules—lowercase, no spaces).

Test it—same look, fraction of the size!

Using Compressed Images

Here's a page with a compressed, responsive image:

```
<!DOCTYPE html>

<html lang="en">

<head>
```

```
    <meta charset="UTF-8">

    <title>Fast Images</title>

    <!-- CSS link -->

    <link rel="stylesheet" href="css/style.css">

</head>

<body>

    <header>

        <h1>My Speedy Site</h1>

    </header>

    <main>

        <section>

            <h2>Beach Day</h2>

            <figure>

                <!-- Compressed and responsive -->

                <img src="images/beach-low.jpg"

                    srcset="images/beach-low.jpg 500w, images/
beach-med.jpg 1000w"

                    sizes="80vw"

                    alt="Compressed beach sunset">

                <figcaption>A sunset, now lightning-fast.</figcaption>

            </figure>

        </section>

    </main>

</body>

</html>
```

Prep two versions: "beach-low.jpg" (500px, ~50KB) and "beach-med.jpg"
(1000px, ~200KB)—compressed with TinyJPG. Save to "images/" (Chapter 6), test in your browser (Chapter 5)—it's quick and gorgeous.

Checking Your Work

- **File Size**: Right-click the file—KB, not MB? You're golden.

- **Load Time**: Developer tools (Network tab)—under 1 second?
  Sweet.

- **Quality**: Zoom in—blurry edges? Back off compression (e.g., 85% vs. 60%).

Why Compression Rules

- **Speed**: Smaller files = faster loads—crucial for mobile or slow Wi-Fi.

- **Bandwidth**: Less data used—kind to users' plans and your hosting costs.

- **User Happiness**: Quick pages keep visitors—stats say 40% ditch after 3 seconds.

- **SEO**: Google loves fast—compressed images boost you up.

Try It Out

Open an image editor or TinyPNG:

- Take a photo (e.g., "pic.jpg", 2MB), resize to 600px wide.

- Compress to ~100KB—save as "pic-med.jpg".

- Add to "index.html":

```
<img src="images/pic-med.jpg" alt="My fast pic" width="600"
height="400">
```

Test in Chrome or Firefox—check load time in developer tools. Too big? Re-compress at 70%. Add comments (Chapter 10) like

<!-- Compressed hero -->.

Tips for Compression Success

- **Balance**: 70-85% quality often works—test visually.

- **Batch It**: Compress multiple images at once (TinyPNG does 20 free).

- **Format Fit**: JPEG for photos, PNG for graphics (Chapter 17)—don't mix up.

- **Keep Originals**: Save uncompressed versions elsewhere—edit safely.

Chapter 22
Creating Forms (<form>)

You've got visuals dialed in—images sized, responsive, and compressed—and now it's time to let users *do* something on your site. Enter the <form> tag: HTML5's gateway to interactivity, letting people send you messages, sign up, or search your page. Forms collect input—names, emails, choices—and can send it somewhere (like a server, though we'll save that for later). By the end of this chapter, you'll build basic forms that look good and work smart, turning your static pages into two-way streets. Let's get interactive!

What's a Form?

A form is a section where users type, click, or select stuff—think "Contact Us" boxes or login screens. The <form> tag wraps it all, and inside, you add elements like text fields, buttons, and checkboxes. Here's a taste:

```
<form>
    <input type="text" name="username">
    <input type="submit" value="Send">
</form>
```

Test this in your browser (Chapter 5)—you'll see a text box and a button. It won't *do* much yet (no server), but it's a start.

The <form> Tag Basics

- **What It Does**: Groups input elements and defines where their data goes (via action) and how (via method).

- **Key Attributes**:

  o action: URL to send data (e.g., "submit.php"—we'll fake it for now).

o method: How data's sent—get (URL visible) or post (hidden).

Example:

```
<form action="/submit" method="post">
    <p>Enter your name: <input type="text" name="name"></p>
    <input type="submit" value="Submit">
</form>
```

Core Form Elements

Forms need inputs—here's the starter pack:

1. <input>: The Workhorse

- **What**: A self-closing tag for text, buttons, and more—type depends on type.

- **Examples**:

    o Text: <input type="text" name="email">—a box for typing.

    o Submit: <input type="submit" value="Go">—a button to send.

    o name: Labels the input for data collection (e.g., "email" identifies it).

2. <label>: The Guide

- **What**: Links text to an input—click the label, focus the field.

How:

```
<label for="user">Username:</label>
<input type="text" id="user" name="user">
```

o for matches the input's id—accessibility win!

3. *<textarea>: Big Text*

- **What**: A multi-line text box—not self-closing.

Example:

```
<textarea name="message">Type here...</textarea>
```

4.*<button>: Fancy Submit*

- **What**: A clickable button—can replace <input type="submit">.

Example:

```
<button type="submit">Send It</button>
```

A Full Form Example

Here's a contact form with semantic tags (Chapter 11):

```
<!DOCTYPE html>
<html lang="en">
<head>
    <meta charset="UTF-8">
    <title>Form Demo</title>
    <!-- CSS link -->
    <link rel="stylesheet" href="css/style.css">
</head>
<body>
    <header>
        <h1>Contact Me</h1>
    </header>
    <main>
        <section>
            <h2>Get in Touch</h2>
            <!-- Basic contact form -->
```

```
                <form action="/submit" method="post">
            <p>
                <label for="name">Your Name:</label>
                <input type="text" id="name" name="name">
            </p>
            <p>
                <label for="email">Email:</label>
                <input type="email" id="email" name="email">
            </p>
            <p>
                <label for="msg">Message:</label>
                <textarea id="msg" name="message"></textarea>
            </p>
            <button type="submit">Send Message</button>
        </form>
        </section>
    </main>
</body>
</html>
```

Save this as "index.html" (Chapter 6), test it in your browser—you can type, but clicking "Send" won't go anywhere yet (no server). It's functional and semantic!

Why Forms Matter

- **Interactivity**: Users talk back—feedback, sign-ups, searches.

- **Semantics**: <form> and <label> tell assistive tech what's happening—accessibility gold.

- **Engagement**: Forms invite action—key to keeping visitors.

- **Flexibility**: HTML5 adds fancy <input> types (like email)—more on that next.

Chapter 23

Input Types

(<input>, <textarea>, <select>, etc.)

You've got <form> rolling, collecting basic text—now let's spice it up with variety. HTML5's input types—like <input>, <textarea>, and <select>—turn forms into powerhouses, letting users type, pick, or scribble whatever you need. From emails to dropdowns, these elements make your forms flexible and user-friendly. By the end, you'll mix and match inputs to build forms that do more—ready to capture all kinds of data. Let's dive into the options!

Key Input Elements

1. **<input>: The Shape-Shifter**

   o **What**: A self-closing tag with type defining its job.

   o **Examples**:

      ▪ <input type="text" name="name">: Plain text (Chapter 22).

      ▪ <input type="email" name="email">: Email—adds keyboard hints on phones.

      ▪ <input type="password" name="pass">: Hides text—great for logins.

      ▪ <input type="checkbox" name="agree">: Tick boxes—multiple choices.

      ▪ <input type="radio" name="color">: Circles—one choice per name group.

   o **Tip**: name tags data—crucial for submission.

2. **<textarea>: The Big Box**

   o **What**: Multi-line text—not self-closing.

- o **Example**: <textarea name="bio" rows="4" cols="50">Tell me about you...</textarea>—size it with rows and cols.

- o **Why**: Perfect for comments or bios—more space than <input>.

3. **<select>: The Dropdown**

- o **What**: A menu of options—uses <option> tags inside.

- o **Example**:

```
<select name="food">

    <option value="pizza">Pizza</option>

    <option value="tacos">Tacos</option>

</select>
```

- o **Why**: Clean, compact—users pick one (or more with multiple).

A Full Form

```
<!DOCTYPE html>

<html lang="en">

<head>

    <meta charset="UTF-8">

    <title>Input Variety</title>

</head>

<body>

    <main>

        <h1>Sign Up</h1>

        <form action="/submit" method="post">

            <!-- Text and email -->

            <p><label for="name">Name:</label> <input type="text"
id="name" name="name"></p>

            <p><label for="email">Email:</label> <input type="e-
mail" id="email" name="email"></p>

            <!-- Password -->
```

```
            <p><label for="pass">Password:</label> <input type="-
password" id="pass" name="pass"></p>

            <!-- Checkbox -->

            <p><label><input type="checkbox" name="terms"> I
agree</label></p>

            <!-- Radio -->

            <p>Favorite: <label><input type="radio" name="fav"
value="cat"> Cat</label>

                <label><input type="radio" name="fav" val-
ue="dog"> Dog</label></p>

            <!-- Dropdown -->

            <p><label for="color">Color:</label> <select id="col-
or" name="color">

                <option value="red">Red</option>

                <option value="blue">Blue</option>

            </select></p>

            <!-- Textarea -->

            <p><label for="bio">Bio:</label> <textarea id="bio"
name="bio"></textarea></p>

            <input type="submit" value="Join">

        </form>

    </main>

</body>

</html>
```

Sign Up

Name: [   ]

Email: [   ]

Password: [   ]

☐ I agree

Favorite: ○ Cat ○ Dog

Color: [Red ∨]

Bio: [   ]

[Join]

Save as "index.html" (Chapter 6), test in your browser (Chapter 5)—type, click, pick, and play!

- **Variety**: Match inputs to data—emails get type="email", choices get <select>.

- **Semantics**: <label> and type boost accessibility—screen readers love it.

- **User-Friendly**: Keyboards adapt (e.g., @ for email) on mobile.

Try It

Tweak your "index.html" in your text editor (Chapter 4):

- Add <input type="password">, <select> with 3 options, and <textarea>.

- Test in Chrome—click checkboxes, pick radio, type away.

Add comments (Chapter 10) like <!-- User choices -->. Explore—swap text for tel (phone numbers)!

Chapter 24
Form Validation with HTML5

Forms are talking, but what if users type gibberish? HTML5's built-in validation catches bad input—like fake emails or empty fields—before submission, no JavaScript needed yet. It's like a bouncer for your data, keeping it clean and useful. By the end, you'll add validation to your forms, making them smart and sturdy. Let's guard the gates!

Validation Basics

- **Attributes**:

    o required: Must be filled—<input type="text" required>.

    o pattern: Matches a regex—e.g., <input type="text" pattern="[A-Za-z]+"> (letters only).

    • min/max: Numbers or dates—<input type="number" min="1" max="10">.

- **Types Help**: type="email" auto-checks for @—no pattern needed.

Example Form

```
<form action="/submit" method="post">
    <p><label for="email">Email:</label>
        <input type="email" id="email" name="email" required></p>
    <p><label for="age">Age:</label>
        <input type="number" id="age" name="age" min="13"
max="99" required></p>
    <p><label for="code">Code (3 letters):</label>
        <input type="text" id="code" name="code" pat-
tern="[A-Za-z]{3}" required></p>
    <input type="submit" value="Go">
</form>
```

Test it—leave email blank (error!), type "abc@" (invalid!), or "12" for age (too low!). Browsers pop up messages—free validation!

Why It's Great

- **Ease**: No coding—just attributes.

- **Feedback**: Browsers warn users—e.g., "Please fill out this field."

- **Accessibility**: Screen readers catch errors too.

- **Prevention**: Stops junk data early.

Try It

Add to your "index.html":

- Make email <input type="email" required>.

- Add <input type="number" min="1" required> for quantity.

- Test—submit blank or wrong, see the magic.

Comment it—<!-- Validated email -->. Play—try type="url" with required!

Chapter 25
Buttons and Submission

Forms are validated—now let's finish strong with buttons and submission. The <button> and <input type="submit"> tags trigger action, sending user data where it needs to go (or faking it for now). By the end, you'll craft buttons that work and look good, tying your form together. Let's hit submit!

Buttons Basics

1. **<input type="submit">:**

   o Simple, self-closing—<input type="submit" value="Send">.

   o Text in value—default action is form submit.

2. **<button>:**

   o Flexible—<button type="submit">Go!</button>—content between tags.

   o Types: submit (default), reset (clears form), button (custom later).

Example

```
<form action="/submit" method="post">

    <p><label for="name">Name:</label> <input type="text"
id="name" name="name" required></p>

    <!-- Two submit options -->

    <input type="submit" value="Submit Now">

    <button type="submit">Send It!</button>

    <!-- Reset option -->

    <button type="reset">Clear</button>

</form>
```

Test it—type a name, click either submit (no server, so refresh), or reset to wipe it.

Why It Matters

- **Action**: Buttons launch the form—data's useless without them.
- **Style**: <button> takes images or text—CSS will love it.
- **Control**: reset or multiple buttons (e.g., "Save Draft") add options.

Try It

Tweak your form:

- Add <button type="submit">Go</button> and <input type="submit" value="Send">.
- Toss in <button type="reset">Start Over</button>.
- Test—submit, reset, repeat.

Comment—<!-- Form buttons -->. Experiment—add <img> inside <button>!

Chapter 26
Adding Videos with <video>

You've got forms collecting input—now let's add some pizzazz with videos. The <video> tag brings moving pictures to your HTML5 pages, no plugins needed (goodbye, Flash!). It's semantic, flexible, and built for the modern web. By the end, you'll embed videos that play right in your browser. Let's roll the tape!

The <video> Tag

- **What**: Embeds video files—self-contained, not a link.

- **Key Attributes**: src (file path), controls (play buttons—next chapter).

Example:

```
<video src="videos/clip.mp4"></video>
```

Add to your "videos" folder (Chapter 6)—won't play yet without controls.

A Full Example

```
<!DOCTYPE html>
<html lang="en">
<head>
    <meta charset="UTF-8">
    <title>Video Demo</title>
</head>
<body>
    <main>
        <h1>My Video</h1>
```

```
        <section>
            <h2>Watch This</h2>
            <!-- Basic video -->
            <video src="videos/sample.mp4" controls></video>
            <p>A short clip I made.</p>
        </section>
    </main>
</body>
</html>
```

Grab a small MP4 (e.g., from sample-videos.com), save as "sample.mp4" in "videos/," test in your browser (Chapter 5)—play it!

My Video

Watch This

A short clip I made.

Why It's Cool

- **Native**: No external players—HTML5 handles it.

- **Semantics**: Pairs with <figure> (Chapter 18) for captions.

- **Flexibility**: Add options next—controls, autoplay, more.

Try It

Tweak "index.html" in your text editor (Chapter 4):

- Add <video src="videos/yourclip.mp4" controls>.

- Test—play, pause, enjoy.

Add comments (Chapter 10)—<!-- My first video -->. Next, we'll tweak it!

Chapter 27

Supported Formats and Codecs

Videos are in—now let's ensure they work everywhere. The <video> tag supports specific formats and codecs—file types and compression tech—that browsers understand. Pick wrong, and it's a blank screen. By the end, you'll know the safe bets and how to cover all bases. Let's decode it!

Formats and Codecs

- **MP4 (H.264)**: The gold standard—works in Chrome, Firefox, Safari.

- **WebM (VP8/VP9)**: Open-source, great quality—Chrome and Firefox love it.

- **OGG (Theora)**: Less common—older support.

Multiple Sources

Browsers differ—use <source> inside <video>:

```
<video controls>
    <source src="videos/clip.mp4" type="video/mp4">
    <source src="videos/clip.webm" type="video/webm">
    Your browser doesn't support video.
</video>
```

- type: MIME type—helps the browser pick.

- Fallback text: Shows if no format works.

Example

```
<video controls>
    <source src="videos/sample.mp4" type="video/mp4">
```

```
    <source src="videos/sample.webm" type="video/webm">
    Sorry, no video support!
</video>
```

Convert "sample.mp4" to WebM (try HandBrake or online tools), test—plays anywhere!

Why It Matters

- **Compatibility**: MP4 + WebM = 95%+ browser coverage.

- **Efficiency**: Codecs shrink files—faster loads (Chapter 21).

Try It

Add <source> tags to your <video>—test MP4 and WebM. Comment—<!-- Multi-format video -->.

Chapter 28
Adding Controls, Autoplay, and Looping

Videos play—now let's make them user-friendly or dynamic with controls, autoplay, and loop. These attributes tweak how <video> behaves, from manual play to auto-repeats. By the end, you'll customize playback like a director. Let's cue it up!

Attributes

- controls: Adds play/pause, volume—<video controls>.

- autoplay: Starts on load—<video autoplay> (muted often required).

- loop: Repeats—<video loop>.

Example

```
<video controls autoplay loop muted>
    <source src="videos/loop.mp4" type="video/mp4">
</video>
```

- muted: Silences for autoplay—browsers block loud auto-starts.

Why It's Handy

- **Usability**: controls empowers users.

- **Engagement**: autoplay grabs attention (e.g., backgrounds).

- **Effect**: loop suits short clips—think GIFs.

Try It

Tweak your video—add controls, autoplay, loop. Test—mute if it won't auto-play. Comment—<!-- Looping clip -->.

Chapter 29
Using Poster Images

Videos can look blah before playing—enter the poster attribute, a static image placeholder. It's like a movie poster, teasing the action. By the end, you'll give your <video> a stylish start screen. Let's set the scene!

The poster Attribute

- **What**: Shows an image before play—<video poster="images/poster.jpg">.

Example:

```
<video controls poster="images/scene.jpg">

    <source src="videos/sample.mp4" type="video/mp4">

</video>
```

Save a frame as "scene.jpg" (Chapter 17)—test, see it pre-play.

Why It's Neat

- **Appeal**: Looks pro—not a black box.

- **Hint**: Teases content—entices clicks.

Try It

Add poster="images/yourpic.jpg"—compress it (Chapter 21), test. Comment—<!-- Video teaser -->.

Chapter 30
Adding Audio with <audio>

Videos rock—now let's add sound with <audio>. It's <video>'s lean cousin, perfect for music or podcasts. By the end, you'll embed audio that hums along. Let's tune in!

The <audio> Tag

- **What**: Plays sound—<audio src="audio/song.mp3">.

Example:

```
<audio controls>

    <source src="audio/sample.mp3" type="audio/mp3">

</audio>
```

Grab an MP3, test—play it!

Formats

- MP3: Universal.

- OGG, WAV: Alternatives—use <source>.

Why It's Great

- **Lightweight**: Audio-only—less bandwidth.

- **Versatile**: Background tunes or narration.

Try It

Add <audio controls> with an MP3—test. Comment—<!-- My soundtrack -->.

Chapter 31
Embedding YouTube Videos
and Other External Media

Local media's cool—now let's tap YouTube or others with embeds. No hosting needed—just an <iframe>. By the end, you'll pull in external clips effortlessly. Let's stream it!

The <iframe> Tag

- **What**: Embeds external content—<iframe src="youtube.com/em-bed/VIDEO_ID">.

Example:

```
<iframe width="560" height="315" src="https://www.youtube.com/em-
bed/dQw4w9WgXcQ" frameborder="0"></iframe>
```

Copy a YouTube "Embed" code—test it!

Why It's Easy

- **No Upload**: Use others' hosting.

- **Rich**: Video, maps, tweets—<iframe> does it.

Try It

Embed a YouTube video—resize with width/height. Comment—<!--Rickroll -->.

Chapter 32
Creating a Simple Image Gallery

Multimedia's flowing—now let's showcase photos in a gallery. Using <img> and <figure> (Chapters 17-18), you'll build a grid. By the end, you'll have a visual showcase. Let's snap it together!

Gallery Example

```
<main>
    <h1>My Gallery</h1>
    <section>
        <figure>
            <img src="images/pic1.jpg" alt="Pic 1" width="200">
            <figcaption>Day 1</figcaption>
        </figure>
        <figure>
            <img src="images/pic2.jpg" alt="Pic 2" width="200">
            <figcaption>Day 2</figcaption>
        </figure>
    </section>
</main>
```

Add compressed pics (Chapter 21)—test, tweak sizes!

Why It Works

- **Simple**: <figure> organizes—CSS will grid it later.

- **Scalable**: Add more <figure>s—grows easy.

Try It

Build a 3-image gallery—test. Comment—<!-- Photo grid -->.

Chapter 33
Adding a Lightbox Effect
for Pop-Up Images

Gallery's up—now let's make it pop with a lightbox: click an image, it zooms fullscreen. HTML5 alone can't do it (needs JavaScript), but we'll prep with structure. By the end, you'll set the stage—CSS/JS next. Let's zoom in!

Prep Example

```
<main>
    <h1>Lightbox Gallery</h1>
    <section>
        <a href="images/pic1-big.jpg" class="lightbox">
            <img src="images/pic1.jpg" alt="Pic 1" width="200">
        </a>
        <a href="images/pic2-big.jpg" class="lightbox">
            <img src="images/pic2.jpg" alt="Pic 2" width="200">
        </a>
    </section>
</main>
```

Add big versions (e.g., "pic1-big.jpg")—click opens raw images for now.

Why It's Prep

- **Structure**: <a> links to big pics—JS will intercept.

- **Engagement**: Pop-ups immerse—CSS styles later.

Try It

Set up 2 linked images—test clicks. Comment—<!-- Lightbox ready -->.

Chapter 34

What is CSS?

Imagine you're building a house. You've got the foundation and the walls up—thanks to some sturdy bricks and mortar—but it's still just a gray, boxy structure. No one's going to stop and admire it. Now, picture adding a fresh coat of paint, hanging curtains, and planting a garden out front. Suddenly, it's not just a house; it's a *home*. In the world of websites, that foundation is HTML—HyperText Markup Language, the structure that holds everything together. But the paint, the curtains, the charm? That's CSS.

CSS stands for **Cascading Style Sheets**, and it's the magic wand of web design. While HTML gives a webpage its bones—defining headings, paragraphs, images, and links—CSS dresses it up. It controls how everything *looks*: the colors, fonts, layouts, and even subtle animations that make a site feel alive. Without CSS, the internet would be a sea of plain text on white backgrounds—functional, sure, but about as exciting as a blank wall.

So, how does it work? CSS is a language of rules. You write instructions that tell a browser—like Chrome or Firefox—how to style the elements HTML has laid out. For example, you might say, "Make all my headings bright blue," or "Put a gray border around my images." These rules cascade—hence the name—meaning they flow down through the page, applying styles in a specific order based on how you've written them. If you tell the browser that all text should be green but then specify that paragraphs should be purple, the paragraphs will win out because more specific rules take priority. It's like a game of rock-paper-scissors, but for design.

Let's break it down with an example. Imagine you've got a simple webpage with this HTML:

```
<h1>Welcome to My Site</h1>
<p>This is my first webpage!</p>
```

Without CSS, it's just black text on a white background, sized by the browser's default settings. Now, add some CSS:

```
h1 {

  color: teal;

  font-size: 36px;

  text-align: center;

}


p {

  color: darkgray;

  font-family: Arial;

  line-spacing: 1.5;

}
```

Suddenly, your heading is a bold teal, centered at the top, and your paragraph is a sleek dark gray in a clean Arial font with comfy spacing. That's CSS at work—taking the raw material of HTML and turning it into something polished.

One of the coolest things about CSS is its flexibility. You can apply styles in a few ways. You might write them directly in your HTML file (inline CSS), but that's like painting one room at a time—tedious and hard to change later. More commonly, you'll use a separate CSS file (external CSS) linked to your HTML, letting you style an entire site consistently with one set of rules. There's also the <style> tag within HTML (internal CSS), a middle ground for smaller projects. This separation of structure (HTML) and style (CSS) is a big deal—it keeps things organized and makes updates a breeze.

CSS has evolved over the years. Back in the 1990s, when the web was young, sites relied on clunky tricks like tables and invisible images to control layouts. CSS, first proposed by Håkon Wium Lie in 1994 and standardized by 1996, changed all that. Today, it's a powerhouse. With modern CSS, you can create responsive designs that adapt to phones, tablets, and desktops, animate elements like a Pixar movie, and even build complex grids that once required heavy coding.

Why should you care? Because CSS is everywhere. Every sleek website, every colorful button, every smooth hover effect—it's all CSS. Whether you're a hobbyist tinkering with a blog or a business owner crafting a brand, understanding CSS unlocks creativity. It's not just code; it's the art of making the digital world beautiful.

Chapter 35
Inline, Internal, and External CSS

CSS is your style key—now let's unlock *how* to apply it. There are three ways: inline (on a tag), internal (in <head>), and external (a separate file). Each has its place, from quick fixes to site-wide rules. By the end, you'll know when to use each and start styling your HTML5 pages. Let's layer it on!

1. Inline CSS

- **What**: Style right in the tag with style="".

Example:

HTML:

```
<p style="color: red;">Red text!</p>
```

- **Pros**: Fast for one-off tweaks—test in your <img> (Chapter 17).
- **Cons**: Messy for lots of elements—no reuse.

2. Internal CSS

- **What**: Rules in <style> inside <head>—one page only.

Example:

HTML:

```
<head>
    <meta charset="UTF-8">
    <title>Internal CSS</title>
    <style>
```

```
        h1 { color: green; }

        p { font-size: 18px; }

    </style>

</head>

<body>

    <h1>Green Heading</h1>

    <p>Bigger text here.</p>

</body>
```

- **Pros**: Good for single pages—keeps it contained.
- **Cons**: Repeats if you've got multiple pages.

3. External CSS

- **What**: A separate .css file linked with <link> (Chapter 8).

Example:

HTML:

```
<head>

    <meta charset="UTF-8">

    <title>External CSS</title>
```

```
        <link rel="stylesheet" href="css/style.css">
</head>
```

In "css/style.css" (Chapter 6's folder):

CSS:

```
h1 { color: blue; }
p { text-align: center; }
```

- **Pros**: Rules all pages—edit once, style everywhere.
- **Cons**: Extra file to manage—worth it!

Why These Options?

- Inline: Quick tests (e.g., <video> borders—Chapter 26).
- Internal: One-off pages (e.g., a form—Chapter 22).
- External: Full sites (e.g., gallery—Chapter 32).

Try It

In your text editor (Chapter 4):

- Inline: Add <p style="color: purple;">Purple!</p>.
- Internal: Add <style> to <head>—style <h1>.
- External: Create "css/style.css," link it, style <p>.

Test in your browser—see the cascade! Comment—<!-- CSS test -->.

Chapter 36
CSS Syntax and Selectors

CSS is hooked up—now let's write it right. CSS syntax is simple: rules with selectors (what to style) and declarations (how). Selectors target HTML—like <h1> or custom classes—giving you pinpoint control. By the end, you'll craft rules to style your HTML5 pages with precision. Let's select and style!

CSS Syntax

- **Rule**: selector { property: value; }

Example:

CSS:

```
p {
    color: red;
    font-size: 16px;
}
```

- o   p: Selector—targets all <p> tags.

- o   color, font-size: Properties—what changes.

- o   red, 16px: Values—how it changes.

Key Selectors

1. **Element**: Targets tags—h1 { color: blue; } hits all <h1>s.

2. **Class**: .class-name {}—add class="class-name" to HTML:

HTML:

```
<p class="highlight">This is special.</p>
```

CSS:

```
.highlight { background: yellow; }
```

3. **ID**: #id-name {}—unique, one element:

HTML:

```
<p id="intro">Start here.</p>
```

CSS:

```
#intro { font-weight: bold; }
```

Example Page

HTML:

```
<!DOCTYPE html>
<html lang="en">
<head>
    <meta charset="UTF-8">
    <title>CSS Selectors</title>
    <link rel="stylesheet" href="css/style.css">
</head>
<body>
    <h1 class="title">My Site</h1>
    <p id="intro">Welcome!</p>
```

```
      <p class="highlight">Check this out.</p>
</body>
</html>
```

In "css/style.css":

```
h1 { color: green; }
.title { font-size: 24px; }
#intro { text-align: center; }
.highlight { background: yellow; }
```

Test it—green heading, big title, centered intro, yellow highlight!

Why It's Powerful

- **Precision**: Selectors target exactly what you want—<form> inputs (Chapter 22) or gallery <img>s (Chapter 32).

- **Reuse**: Classes style multiple elements—efficiency!

- **Hierarchy**: Rules cascade—element, class, ID (specificity grows).

Try It

In "css/style.css":

- Style all <p>—p { color: blue; }.

- Add <p class="note"> and .note { font-style: italic; }.

- Use `<h1 id="main">` and `#main { border: 1px solid black; }`.

Test in your browser—layer the styles! Comment—`<!-- Selector styles -->`.

Chapter 37
Changing Font Family, Size, and Weight

You've built a solid HTML5 foundation—paragraphs, headings, forms, images, and videos—all structured and functional. But let's be honest: without styling, they're stuck in the browser's default look—black Times New Roman on white, like a 1990s word processor. That's where CSS swoops in, and today, we're starting with the text itself. The font-family, font-size, and font-weight properties let you shape how your words appear, turning plain <p> tags into eye-catching prose or bold <h1> titles into commanding headlines. By the end of this chapter, you'll transform your pages' typography, making them readable, stylish, and yours. Let's dive into the art of text!

What These Properties Do

CSS gives you control over three key aspects of text:

- **font-family**: Picks the typeface—Arial, Times, or something wilder. It's like choosing the voice your site speaks in.

- **font-size**: Sets how big or small the text is—pixels (px), ems, or keywords like large. Think of it as adjusting the volume.

- **font-weight**: Controls thickness—normal, bold, or numbers (100 to 900). It's the emphasis knob, dialing up impact.

Together, they turn <h1>My Site</h1> from default drab to a custom vibe—say, a sleek sans-serif at 24px, bold as brass.

Getting Started

Let's assume you're using external CSS (Chapter 35)—your "css/style.css" linked via <link> in "index.html" (Chapter 6). Here's a starter:

CSS:

```
h1 {
    font-family: Arial, sans-serif;
    font-size: 24px;
```

```
    font-weight: bold;

}

p {

    font-family: Georgia, serif;

    font-size: 16px;

    font-weight: normal;

}
```

Add this to "style.css," then tweak your HTML:
HTML:

```
<h1>My Site</h1>
<p>Welcome to my world of web design.</p>
```

Open it in your browser (Chapter 5)—the <h1> is now Arial, bigger, and bold, while <p> rocks a classic Georgia at a comfy 16px. That's the power of CSS!

Digging Deeper: font-family

The font-family property takes a list—e.g., Arial, sans-serif—because not all devices have every font. Arial's the first choice; if it's missing, the browser picks a sans-serif fallback. Options include:

- **Serif**: Fancy tails (e.g., Times New Roman)—traditional, bookish.

- **Sans-serif**: Clean lines (e.g., Helvetica)—modern, web-friendly.

- **Monospace**: Fixed-width (e.g., Courier)—code-like, retro.

Try font-family: "Courier New", monospace; on <p>—it's typewriter chic!

Sizing with font-size

Pixels (px) are precise—16px is a web standard for body text. But you can go big (32px for headings) or small (12px for fine print). Keywords work too—small, medium, large—though they're less exact. For your <form> labels (Chapter 22), font-size: 14px; keeps them clear without shouting.

normal (400) is default; bold (700) adds punch. Numbers (100-900, steps of 100) offer nuance—if the font supports it (Arial does, some don't). Test font-weight: 600; on <h1>—it's hefty but not full bold.

Real-World Example

Let's style a page with your gallery (Chapter 32):

HTML:

```
<main>
    <h1>My Photo Gallery</h1>
    <section>
        <figure>
            <img src="images/pic1.jpg" alt="Pic 1" width="200">
            <figcaption>First snap</figcaption>
        </figure>
    </section>
</main>
```

CSS:

```
h1 {
    font-family: "Helvetica", sans-serif;
    font-size: 28px;
    font-weight: 700;
}
figcaption {
    font-family: "Times New Roman", serif;
    font-size: 14px;
    font-weight: normal;
}
```

The <h1> stands tall; <figcaption> feels elegant—typography with purpose.

My Photo Gallery

First snap

Why It Matters

- **Readability**: 16px text beats tiny defaults—users stay comfy (Chapter 13's <p>).

- **Branding**: Fonts set tone—sleek for tech, serif for stories.

- **Hierarchy**: Bigger, bolder <h1> (Chapter 12) grabs eyes first.

Hands-On Practice

Open your text editor (Chapter 4), tweak "style.css":

- Set <h1> to font-family: "Verdana", sans-serif; font-size: 30px; font-weight: bold;.

- Make <p> font-family: "Garamond", serif; font-size: 18px; font-weight: 400;.

- Add a <figcaption> (Chapter 18)—style it font-size: 12px;.

Test in Chrome or Firefox—resize the window, zoom in/out (Ctrl +/-). Does it feel balanced? Add comments (Chapter 10)—<!-- Styled headings -->. Experiment: swap bold for 500, try "Courier" on <p>—see what sticks!

What's Next

Fonts are just the start—next, we'll align and decorate text, then fetch fancier ones from Google. Your <form> (Chapter 22), <video> captions (Chapter 26), and gallery (Chapter 32) are about to get a typographic glow-up!

Chapter 38
Text Alignment and Decoration

Your fonts are singing with family, size, and weight—now let's position and polish them. The text-align and text-decoration properties in CSS control where text sits (left, right, center) and how it's adorned (underlined, struck through). These tweaks make your <h1> headings pop, your <p> paragraphs flow, and your <a> links stand out. By the end, you'll align your content like a designer and decorate it with flair, turning your HTML5 pages into visual stories. Let's line it up and dress it up!

text-align: Positioning Text

- **What**: Moves text horizontally—left (default), right, center, justify.

- **How**: Applies to block elements (e.g., <p>, <h1>)—inline like <span> ignores it.

Example:

```
h1 { text-align: center; }
p { text-align: justify; }
```

<h1> centers—grand and proud; <p> spreads evenly—book-like.

Text-decoration: Adding Flair

- **What**: Adds lines—underline, overline, line-through, or none (removes defaults).

- **How**: Works on any text—great for <a> (Chapter 15) or emphasis.

```
a { text-decoration: none; }
.strike { text-decoration: line-through; }
```

Links lose underlines; .strike class crosses out text.

Combining Them

Here's a styled snippet:

HTML:

```
<h1>Welcome</h1>

<p>A long paragraph to justify and see how it wraps across lines
nicely.</p>

<a href="https://example.com" class="fancy">Click me</a>
```

CSS:

```
h1 {

    text-align: center;

    text-decoration: underline;

}
p {

    text-align: justify;

}
.fancy {

    text-decoration: overline;

}
```

Test it (Chapter 5)—<h1> is centered with a line below, <p> fills the width, <a> gets a top line—stylish yet readable.

Deep Dive: text-align

- **Left**: Web default—good for most <p> (Chapter 13).

- **Right**: Rare—try it on <figcaption> (Chapter 18) for artsy captions.

- **Center**: Bold move—perfect for <h1> (Chapter 12) or <button> text (Chapter 25).

- **Justify**: Spreads text—elegant for long <section> content (Chapter 11), but watch for awkward gaps.

Deep Dive: text-decoration

- **Underline**: Classic—highlight <a> or <strong> (Chapter 9).

- **Line-through**: Strikethrough—mark old <p> prices or tasks.

- **Overline**: Quirky—try on <span> (future chapter) for flair.

- **None**: Strips <a> underlines—clean, modern links.

Practical Application

Style your gallery (Chapter 32):

HTML:

```
<main>
    <h1>My Photos</h1>
    <figure>
        <img src="images/pic1.jpg" alt="Pic 1" width="200">
        <figcaption>First adventure</figcaption>
    </figure>
</main>
```

CSS:

```
h1 {
    text-align: center;
    text-decoration: underline;
}
figcaption {
    text-align: right;
    text-decoration: none;
}
```

The title's a centered statement; captions hug the right—subtle elegance.

Why It's Essential

- **Flow**: text-align organizes—e.g., center <form> labels (Chapter 22).

- **Emphasis**: text-decoration draws eyes—e.g., underline <h2> (Chapter 12).

- **Clarity**: Remove <a> underlines—users still know it's clickable with color (next chapter).

Hands-On Practice

In "style.css" (Chapter 35):

- Center <h1>—text-align: center; text-decoration: underline;.

- Justify <p>—text-align: justify;.

- Style <a>—text-decoration: none; and add .highlight { text-decoration: line-through; } to a <p class="highlight">.

Test in your browser—does <h1> feel grand? <p> readable? <a> sleek? Add comments (Chapter 10)—<!-- Aligned title -->. Play: right-align <figcaption>, overline a <span>—see what vibes!

What's Next

Alignment and decoration set the stage—next, Google Fonts bring pro-level typography, then colors splash life into your <video> captions (Chapter 26), <form> buttons (Chapter 25), and beyond!

Chapter 39
Using Google Fonts

Your text's aligned and decorated, with fonts sized and weighted—but the browser's defaults (Arial, Times) feel… basic. What if you want something sharper, cozier, or downright funky? Google Fonts offers hundreds of free, web-ready typefaces, easy to plug into your HTML5 pages with a <link> or CSS tweak. By the end, you'll import and apply Google Fonts, giving your <h1>, <p>, and <form> elements a typographic glow-up that screams personality. Let's fetch some fonts!

What's Google Fonts?

Google Fonts is a library—over 1,000 fonts—hosted online, free to use. No downloads, no installs—just a link, and your site taps into pro typography. From sleek sans-serifs (Roboto) to playful scripts (Lobster), it's a buffet for your font-family.

How to Use It

Two steps:

1. **Link It**: Add a <link> to <head> (Chapter 8).

2. **Apply It**: Set font-family in CSS (Chapter 37).

Visit fonts.google.com, pick a font (say, "Open Sans"):

- Click "Select this style" (e.g., Regular 400, Bold 700).

- Copy the <link>:

HTML:

```
<link href="https://fonts.googleapis.com/css2?family=Open+Sans:wght@400;700&display=swap" rel="stylesheet">
```

- Add to "index.html":

HTML:

```
<head>
    <meta charset="UTF-8">
    <title>Font Fun</title>
    <link href="https://fonts.googleapis.com/css2?fami-
ly=Open+Sans:wght@400;700&display=swap" rel="stylesheet">
    <link rel="stylesheet" href="css/style.css">
</head>
```

In "style.css":

```
body {
    font-family: "Open Sans", sans-serif;
}
h1 {
    font-weight: 700; /* Bold */
}
p {
    font-weight: 400; /* Regular */
}
```

Test it—<h1> and <p> now rock Open Sans, crisp and modern!

Alternative: @import

Instead of <link>, add to "style.css":

```
@import url('https://fonts.googleapis.com/css2?fami-
ly=Open+Sans:wght@400;700&display=swap');
body {
    font-family: "Open Sans", sans-serif;
}
```

Same result—<link> is lighter, but @import keeps CSS tidy.

Picking Fonts

- **Sans-serif**: "Roboto," "Lato"—clean, web-friendly.

- **Serif**: "Merriweather," "Playfair Display"—elegant, story-like.

- **Display**: "Lobster," "Pacifico"—wild, sparingly for <h1>.

Pair them—e.g., "Roboto" for <p>, "Lobster" for <h1>—but limit to two for harmony.

Full Example

Style your form (Chapter 22):

HTML:

```
<!DOCTYPE html>
<html lang="en">
<head>
    <meta charset="UTF-8">
    <title>Google Fonts</title>
    <link href="https://fonts.googleapis.com/css2?family=Roboto-
:wght@400&family=Lobster&display=swap" rel="stylesheet">
    <link rel="stylesheet" href="css/style.css">
</head>
<body>
    <main>
        <h1>Contact Me</h1>
        <form>
```

```
                <label for="name">Name:</label>
            <input type="text" id="name" name="name">
        </form>
    </main>
</body>
</html>
```

CSS:

```
h1 {
    font-family: "Lobster", cursive;
    font-size: 32px;
    font-weight: 400;
}
label, input {
    font-family: "Roboto", sans-serif;
    font-size: 16px;
}
```

Test it—<h1> dances in Lobster, <form> stays sharp with Roboto—pro vibes!

Why It's Awesome

- **Free**: No cost, endless options—e.g., <figcaption> (Chapter 18) gets flair.

- **Easy**: <link> beats manual font files—fast setup.

- **Web-Ready**: Optimized—pairs with compression (Chapter 21).

- **Personality**: Your gallery (Chapter 32) or <video> page (Chapter 26) reflects *you*.

Hands-On Practice

Visit fonts.google.com:

- Pick "Poppins" (400, 700)—add <link> to <head>.

- In "style.css":

  o <h1>: font-family: "Poppins", sans-serif; font-size: 28px; font-weight: 700;.

  o <p>: font-family: "Poppins", sans-serif; font-size: 16px; font-weight: 400;.

  o <a> (Chapter 15): font-family: "Poppins", sans-serif;.

Test in your browser—refresh, zoom, check mobile (Chapter 5). Add comments—<!-- Google Fonts added -->. Play: try "Montserrat" for <h1>, "Source Sans Pro" for <p>—mix and match!

Chapter 40
Setting Colors
(Hex, RGB, HSL)

Your text's got style—fonts, sizes, alignment—all thanks to CSS. But it's still stuck in black-and-white land, like an old movie begging for color. The color property in CSS is your palette, splashing vibrancy onto your <h1> headings, <p> paragraphs, <a> links, and more. With three main ways to set it—hex codes, RGB, and HSL—you'll paint your HTML5 pages with precision and personality. By the end of this chapter, you'll turn your forms, galleries, and videos into a visual feast, mastering color like a web artist. Let's mix some hues!

What's the color Property?

The color property sets the foreground color—usually text—of any HTML element. It works with selectors (Chapter 36) to target <h1>, <p>, or classes. You've got three big tools:

- **Hex Codes**: Six-digit codes (e.g., #FF0000 for red)—web classic.

- **RGB**: Red, Green, Blue values (0-255, e.g., rgb(255, 0, 0)—also red).

- **HSL**: Hue, Saturation, Lightness (e.g., hsl(0, 100%, 50%)—red again)—intuitive for tweaking.

Each method's a different brush—hex is quick, RGB is familiar, HSL is adjustable. Let's paint!

Hex Codes: The Web Standard

Hex starts with # followed by six characters—two each for red, green, blue (00-FF in hexadecimal). #000000 is black; #FFFFFF is white; #FF0000 is pure red. Shorten to three for simples—#F00 is still red.

CSS:

```
h1 { color: #0066CC; }  /* Blue-ish */

p { color: #333333; }  /* Dark gray */
```

Add to "style.css" (Chapter 35), test with:

```
<h1>My Site</h1>

<p>Welcome to color town!</p>
```

Open in your browser (Chapter 5)—<h1> glows blue, <p> softens to gray.

RGB: Mixing Like Paint

RGB uses numbers (0-255) for red, green, blue—think digital art class. rgb(255, 0, 0) is red; rgb(0, 255, 0) is green; rgb(0, 0, 255) is blue.

Example:
CSS:

```
a { color: rgb(255, 165, 0); }  /* Orange links */
```

Pair with <a href="#" class="fancy">Click me</a>—orange pops against default blue (Chapter 15).

HSL: Hue, Saturation, Lightness

HSL is human-friendly—hue (0-360° on a color wheel), saturation (0-100% intensity), lightness (0-100% brightness). hsl(120, 100%, 50%) is vivid green; hsl(120, 50%, 75%) is pastel.

Example:
HTML:

```
figcaption { color: hsl(240, 80%, 60%); }  /* Bright blue */
```

178

Use with <figcaption> (Chapter 18)—tweak 50% to 70% for lighter shades.

Practical Application

Color your gallery (Chapter 32):

HTML:

```
<main>
    <h1>My Photos</h1>
    <section>
        <figure>
            <img src="images/pic1.jpg" alt="Pic 1" width="200">
            <figcaption>Summer snap</figcaption>
        </figure>
    </section>
</main>
```

CSS:

```
h1 {
    color: #8A2BE2; /* Deep purple */
    font-family: "Open Sans", sans-serif; /* Chapter 39 */
}
figcaption {
    color: rgb(0, 128, 128); /* Teal */
    font-size: 14px;
}
a {
    color: hsl(0, 80%, 50%); /* Bright red */
}
```

Test it—<h1> commands in purple, <figcaption> cools in teal, <a> links flare red. Colors tie visuals to text!

Why Colors Matter

- **Mood**: Purple <h1> feels bold—e.g., <video> pages (Chapter 26).

- **Readability**: Dark gray <p> (e.g., #333) beats black on white—eases eyes (Chapter 13).

- **Branding**: Red <a> links match a logo—consistency (Chapter 19's <img>).

- **Engagement**: Bright <button> text (Chapter 25) screams "Click me!"

Hands-On Practice

In "style.css":

- <h1>: color: #FF4500; (orange-red)—bold title.

- <p>: color: rgb(70, 130, 180); (steel blue)—calm body.

- <a>: color: hsl(300, 70%, 40%); (magenta)—vibrant links.

- Add <figcaption class="note"> and .note { color: #228B22; } (forest green).

Test in your browser—refresh, zoom (Ctrl +/-), check contrast. Does <h1> pop? <p> soothe? Add comments (Chapter 10)—<!-- Colorful text -->. Experiment: try #FFD700 (gold) on <h1>, rgb(128, 0, 128) (purple) on <p>, hsl(60, 100%, 50%) (yellow) on <a>—find your vibe!

Tools and Tips

- **Pickers**: Use Chrome DevTools (right-click > Inspect > Styles > color box) or online tools (coolors.co).

- **Contrast**: Dark text on light backgrounds—#FFF on #000 strains; #333 on #F5F5F5 rocks.

- **Fallback**: Browsers get hex, RGB, HSL—stick to these (no "red" keywords yet).

What's Next

Colors light up your text—next, backgrounds paint the canvas behind your <form> (Chapter 22), <video> (Chapter 26), and gallery (Chapter 32). Your web's about to glow!

Chapter 41
Background Colors and Images

Text's colorful now, but the page itself? Still a blank slate. The background-color and background-image properties in CSS let you paint behind your HTML5 elements—<body>, <section>, <div>—turning empty space into a mood-setting backdrop. From solid hues to photos, you'll layer depth and style onto your forms, galleries, and videos. By the end, you'll master backgrounds, making your pages pop with personality and polish. Let's fill the void!

background-color: Solid Hues

- **What**: Sets a solid color behind an element—hex, RGB, HSL (Chapter 40).

- **How**: Applies to any block (e.g., <main>) or inline with padding (e.g., <span>).

Example:

```
body { background-color: #F0F0F0; } /* Light gray */

h1 { background-color: rgb(255, 215, 0); } /* Gold */
```

Add to "style.css," test:

```
<h1>My Site</h1>
```

<body> softens to gray; <h1> glows gold behind text.

background-image: Pictures

- **What**: Layers an image—uses url() with a path (Chapter 17's "images/").

- **How**: Needs size control (next properties) to fit.

Example:

```
section {
  background-image: url('images/pattern.jpg');
}
```

Add a compressed "pattern.jpg" (Chapter 21), test with <section><p>Hi</p></section>—text sits on a patterned backdrop.

Key Helpers

- **background-repeat**: repeat (tiles), no-repeat, repeat-x, repeat-y.

- **background-size**: cover (fills, crops), contain (fits), or 100px 200px.

- **background-position**: top left, center, 50% 50%—where it sits.

Example:

```
main {
  background-image: url('images/bg.jpg');
  background-repeat: no-repeat;
  background-size: cover;
  background-position: center;
}
```

Full Example

Style your gallery (Chapter 32):

```
<main>
    <h1>My Photos</h1>
    <section>
        <figure>
```

```
            <img src="images/pic1.jpg" alt="Pic 1" width="200">
            <figcaption>Summer</figcaption>
        </figure>
    </section>
</main>
```

CSS:

```
body {
    background-color: #E6E6FA; /* Lavender */
}
main {
    background-image: url('images/texture.jpg');
    background-repeat: no-repeat;
    background-size: cover;
    background-position: center;
}
h1 {
    background-color: rgba(255, 99, 71, 0.8); /* Tomato,
semi-transparent */
    color: white;
}
figcaption {
    background-color: #4682B4; /* Steel blue */
    color: #FFF;
}
```

Test it—<body> glows lavender, <main> textures behind, <h1> and <fig-caption> pop with colored blocks. RGBA adds opacity (0-1)—fancy!

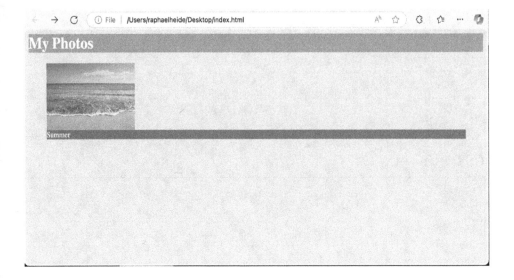

Why Backgrounds Rule

- **Depth**: <body> color sets tone—e.g., <video> page (Chapter 26).

- **Context**: <section> images frame content—e.g., <form> (Chapter 22).

- **Highlight**: <h1> backgrounds draw eyes—e.g., headings (Chapter 12).

- **Branding**: Match <img> tones (Chapter 17)—cohesive style.

Hands-On Practice

In "style.css":

- <body>: background-color: #D3D3D3; (light gray)—subtle base.

- <main>: background-image: url('images/yourbg.jpg'); background-size: cover; background-repeat: no-repeat;.

- <h1>: background-color: rgb(0, 191, 255); color: white; (deep sky blue).

- <p>: background-color: hsl(120, 50%, 90%); (pastel green).

Add to "index.html":

```
<main>
    <h1>Test Page</h1>
    <p>This is colorful!</p>
</main>
```

Test in your browser—resize, check mobile (Chapter 5). Does <main> fill nicely? <h1> stand out? Add comments—<!-- Background styles -->. Play: try #FFDAB9 (peach) on <body>, a pattern image on <section>, rgba(0, 128, 0, 0.5) on <p>—layer it up!

Tips and Tricks

- **Contrast**: White text on dark backgrounds—e.g., #FFF on #4682B4.

- **Optimize**: Compress images (Chapter 21)—fast loads.

- **Fallback**: background-color under background-image—if image fails, color shows.

- **Test**: Zoom, resize—does it hold?

Chapter 42
Introduction to Flexbox

Colors and backgrounds are lighting up your pages, but layout? Still a stack of blocks tumbling down. Enter Flexbox—CSS's flexible box model, a game-changer for arranging elements in rows or columns with display: flex. It's perfect for aligning your gallery <figure>s (Chapter 32), spacing <form> inputs (Chapter 22), or lining up <video> controls (Chapter 26). By the end, you'll wield Flexbox to organize your HTML5 content with ease, making layouts bend to your will. Let's flex some muscle!

What's Flexbox?

Flexbox turns a container (e.g., <div>, <section>) into a flexible parent, arranging its kids (e.g., <p>, <img>) dynamically. Unlike stacking blocks vertically, Flexbox aligns them side-by-side or stacked, adjusting to space. Core idea:

- **Parent**: Gets display: flex—controls the layout.

- **Children**: Flex items—obey the parent's rules.

Basic Setup

Add to "style.css":

```css
.container {
    display: flex;
}
```

HTML:

```html
<div class="container">
    <p>One</p>
    <p>Two</p>
```

```
      <p>Three</p>
</div>
```

Test it—<p> tags line up horizontally, not stacked. That's Flexbox's default—row magic!

Key Properties

- **flex-direction**: row (default), column, row-reverse, column-reverse—sets flow.

- **justify-content**: Spaces items—flex-start, flex-end, center, space-between, space-around.

- **align-items**: Aligns vertically—stretch (default), flex-start, center, baseline.

Example: Gallery Flex

Style your gallery (Chapter 32):

```
<main>
    <h1>My Photos</h1>
    <section class="gallery">
        <figure>
            <img src="images/pic1.jpg" alt="Pic 1" width="200">
            <figcaption>One</figcaption>
        </figure>
        <figure>
            <img src="images/pic2.jpg" alt="Pic 2" width="200">
            <figcaption>Two</figcaption>
        </figure>
    </section>
</main>
```

CSS:

```
.gallery {
    display: flex;
    justify-content: space-around;
    align-items: center;
}
figure {
    background-color: #F5F5F5; /* Light gray */
}
```

Test it—<figure>s spread evenly, centered vertically, with a subtle back-drop. Flexbox aligns like a pro!

Deep Dive

- **Row vs. Column**: flex-direction: column; stacks vertically—try it for <form> inputs (Chapter 22).

- **Spacing**: space-between pushes items to edges; space-around adds even gaps—great for <nav> (Chapter 11).

- **Alignment**: align-items: center; middles items—perfect for <h1> + <p> combos.

Full Flex Example

For your form (Chapter 22):

```html
<form class="flex-form">
    <label for="name">Name:</label>
    <input type="text" id="name" name="name">
    <button type="submit">Send</button>
</form>
```

CSS:

```css
.flex-form {
    display: flex;
    flex-direction: row;
    justify-content: space-between;
    align-items: center;
    background-color: #E0FFFF; /* Light cyan */
    padding: 20px; /* Chapter 43 */
}
label, input, button {
    font-family: "Roboto", sans-serif; /* Chapter 39 */
}
```

Test it—label, input, button line up, spaced nicely, with a cyan frame—form meets Flexbox!

Why Flexbox Rocks

- **Ease**: One line (display: flex) beats float hacks—e.g., <video> rows (Chapter 26).

- **Flexibility**: Adjusts to content—e.g., gallery <figure>s (Chapter 32).

- **Responsiveness**: Gaps and alignment shift—teaser for Chapter 47.

- **Control**: No more <br> hacks (Chapter 13)—layout's king.

Name: [   ]   Send

Hands-On Practice

In "style.css":

- .container { display: flex; justify-content: center; align-items: stretch; }.

- Add <div class="container"><p>A</p><p>B</p><img src="images/pic1.jpg" alt="Pic" width="100"></div>.

- Test—center it. Swap flex-direction: column;, then justify-content: space-evenly;.

Test in your browser—resize, check mobile (Chapter 5). Does it flex? Add comments—<!-- Flex layout -->. Play: try flex-end on <nav> links (Chapter 15), center on <figure>s—bend it!

Tips

- **Width**: Flex items shrink/grow—set width (Chapter 19) if needed.

- **Gaps**: gap: 10px; (modern)—spaces kids cleanly.

- **Test**: Flexbox shines on resize—watch it adapt.

What's Next

Flexbox lays out rows and columns—next, responsive Flexbox (Chapter 47) makes your <form>, <video>, and gallery dance across screens. Your layouts are flexing into the future!

Chapter 43
Linear and Radial Gradients

You've splashed colors and images across your HTML5 pages—text glows, backgrounds hum—but what if you could blend hues into smooth, eye-catching transitions? CSS gradients—linear and radial—let you do just that, turning your <body>, <section>, or <h1> into dynamic canvases with background-image. Forget flat fills; gradients add depth and modernity to your forms, galleries, and videos. By the end of this chapter, you'll craft flowing color shifts that elevate your site's style, making it look like a pro designer's work. Let's gradient-ify your web!

What Are Gradients?

Gradients are background fills that transition between colors—think sunrise fades or glowing buttons. CSS uses background-image (Chapter 41) with two types:

- **Linear**: Colors flow in a straight line—left to right, top to bottom, diagonally.

- **Radial**: Colors radiate from a center—like a spotlight or ripple.

Unlike <img> backgrounds (Chapter 17), gradients are code-generated—no files, instant tweaks.

Linear Gradients: Straight-Line Blends

- **Syntax**: background-image: linear-gradient(direction, color1, color2, ...);

- **Direction**: to right, to bottom, 45deg—where it flows.

Example:

```
body {
    background-image: linear-gradient(to right, #FF6347,
#4682B4);
}
```

Test with <body><h1>Hi</h1></body>—red (#FF6347) fades right to blue (#4682B4).

Radial Gradients: Circular Fades

- **Syntax**: background-image: radial-gradient(shape size at position, color1, color2, ...);

- **Shape**: circle, ellipse (default)—how it spreads.

Example:

```
section {

    background-image: radial-gradient(circle, #FFD700, #228B22);

}
```

Add <section><p>Text</p></section>—gold (#FFD700) radiates to green (#228B22).

Fine-Tuning

- **Color Stops**: linear-gradient(to bottom, red 20%, blue 80%)—red ends at 20%, blue starts at 80%.

- **Multiple Colors**: linear-gradient(45deg, red, yellow, blue)—tri-color diagonal.

- **Position**: radial-gradient(circle at top left, white, gray)—starts top-left.

Practical Example

Style your gallery (Chapter 32):

```
<main>

    <h1>My Photos</h1>

    <section class="gallery">

        <figure>

            <img src="images/pic1.jpg" alt="Pic 1" width="200">

            <figcaption>Summer</figcaption>

        </figure>

    </section>
```

```
</main>
```

CSS in "style.css" (Chapter 35):

```css
body {
    background-image: linear-gradient(to bottom, #87CEEB,
#E0FFFF); /* Sky to cyan */

}
.gallery {
    background-image: radial-gradient(circle at center, #FFB6C1,
#F0E68C); /* Pink to yellow */

    padding: 20px; /* Space for effect */

}
h1 {
    background-image: linear-gradient(to right, #8A2BE2,
#FF69B4); /* Purple to pink */

    color: white;

}
figcaption {
    background-image: radial-gradient(ellipse, #20B2AA, #F5F5F5);
/* Teal to gray */

}
```

Test it (Chapter 5)—<body> flows like a sky, <gallery> radiates warmth, <h1> gradients pop, <figcaption> glows subtly. Colors from Chapter 40 blend seamlessly!

Why Gradients Shine

- **Modernity**: Flat colors feel old—gradients are 2025-ready—e.g., <video> backdrop (Chapter 26).

- **Depth**: <section> gains dimension—e.g., <form> (Chapter 22).

- **No Files**: Unlike <img> (Chapter 17), no compression needed (Chapter 21)—pure CSS.

- **Flexibility**: Tweak hues—e.g., <button> (Chapter 25) hovers.

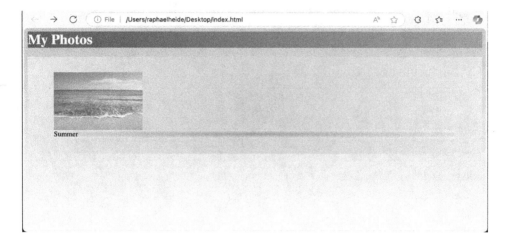

Hands-On Practice

In "style.css":

- <body>: background-image: linear-gradient(to top, #4682B4, #B0C4DE);—blue rises to light blue.

- <main>: background-image: radial-gradient(circle at bottom right, #FF4500, #FFD700);—orange to gold.

- <h1>: background-image: linear-gradient(135deg, #32CD32, #00CED1); color: white;—lime to turquoise, diagonal.

- <p>: background-image: radial-gradient(ellipse, #DDA0DD, #F8F8FF); padding: 10px;—plum to ghost white.

Add to "index.html":

```
<main>
    <h1>Test Gradients</h1>
    <p>This blends beautifully!</p>
</main>
```

Test in your browser—resize, zoom, check mobile. Does <main> radiate? <h1> flow? Add comments (Chapter 10)—<!-- Gradient magic -->. Experiment: try to left on <body>, circle at top on <p>, add a third color (e.g., #8B008B)—blend away!

- **Contrast**: White text on dark gradients—e.g., #FFF on #4682B4.

- **Fallback**: Add background-color: #E0E0E0;—if gradients fail.

- **Test**: Gradients shift on resize—watch edges.

- **Tools**: Use gradient generators (cssgradient.io)—copy-paste ease.

What's Next

Gradients blend your canvas—next, margins and padding (Chapter 43) space your <form>, <video>, and gallery into perfection!

Chapter 44

Understanding Margin, Border, Padding, and Content

Your pages glow with gradients and colors, but everything's smooshed together—text hugs edges, images bump into headings. CSS's box model—margin, border, padding, and content—gives you breathing room and structure. Every HTML element (e.g., <p>, <div>) is a box, and these properties control its layers, spacing your forms, galleries, and videos just right. By the end, you'll master the box model, turning chaos into clean layouts. Let's box it up!

The Box Model Breakdown

Imagine a <p> as a gift box:

- **Content**: The text or <img>—the gift (width/height, Chapter 19).

- **Padding**: Inner wrapping—space between content and border.

- **Border**: The box's edge—visible or not.

- **Margin**: Outer bubble—space outside, pushing neighbors away.

Properties in Action

- **margin**: Outside space—10px, 20px 10px (top/bottom, left/right).

- **border**: Edge style—1px solid black, 2px dashed red.

- **padding**: Inside space—15px, 10px 20px 5px (top, right/left, bottom).

```
p {

    margin: 20px;

    border: 1px solid #4682B4;

    padding: 10px;

}
```

Test with <p>Hi there</p>—20px outside, blue border, 10px inside—spaced and framed!

Shorthand and Specificity

- **Four Values**: margin: 10px 20px 30px 40px;—top, right, bottom, left (clockwise).

- **Two Values**: padding: 15px 25px;—top/bottom, left/right.

- **One Value**: border: 2px solid #FF4500;—uniform orange edge.

Practical Example

Style your form (Chapter 22):

```html
<main>
    <h1>Contact Me</h1>
    <form class="boxy">
        <label for="name">Name:</label>
        <input type="text" id="name" name="name">
    </form>
</main>
```

CSS:

```css
main {
    margin: 30px;
    background-color: #F0F8FF; /* Alice blue */
}
h1 {
    margin: 0 0 20px 0; /* Bottom only */
    padding: 10px;
    border-bottom: 2px solid #FF69B4; /* Pink underline */
}
.boxy {
    padding: 25px;
    border: 1px dashed #20B2AA; /* Teal dashed */
```

```
       background-image: linear-gradient(to right, #E6E6FA, #FFF);
   /* Chapter 42 */
   }
   label {
       margin-right: 10px;
   }
   input {
       padding: 5px;
       border: 1px solid #4682B4;
   }
```

Test it—<main> steps back, <h1> underlines, <form> breathes with padding, <label> and <input> space out—clean and inviting!

Why the Box Model Matters

- **Spacing**: <form> inputs (Chapter 22) don't crowd—margin separates.

- **Structure**: <section> borders (Chapter 11) define areas—e.g., gallery (Chapter 32).

- **Polish**: <h1> padding (Chapter 12) adds cushion—e.g., <video> captions (Chapter 26).

- **Control**: No more <br> hacks (Chapter 13)—layout precision.

In "style.css":

- <body>: margin: 40px; background-color: #F5F5F5;.

- <main>: padding: 30px; border: 2px solid #FFD700;.

- <h1>: margin-bottom: 15px; padding: 10px 20px; border: 1px dashed #32CD32;.

- <p>: margin: 10px 0; padding: 15px; border: 1px solid #FF4500; background-color: #FFF0F5;.

Add to "index.html":

```
<main>
    <h1>Box Test</h1>
    <p>This is spaced out!</p>
</main>
```

Test in your browser—resize, zoom, check mobile. Does <main> frame? <p> breathe? Add comments—<!-- Box model applied -->. Play: try margin: 20px 10px; on <p>, border: 3px dotted #8A2BE2; on <h1>, padding: 5px 15px 25px; on <main>—adjust the layers!

Tips

- **Overlap**: Negative margin (e.g., -10px) pulls closer—test carefully.

- **Collapse**: Vertical margins merge (20px + 20px = 20px)—normal behavior.

- **Visible**: border shows the box—debug with border: 1px solid red;.

What's Next

The box model spaces your world—next, box-sizing (Chapter 44) ensures it behaves, refining your <img> (Chapter 17), <form>, and more!

Chapter 45

Box Sizing and Its Importance

Margins, borders, and padding are shaping your boxes, but something's off—set a <div> to width: 200px, add padding and borders, and it grows fatter than planned. CSS's box-sizing property fixes this, redefining how width and height calculate in the box model (Chapter 43). By the end, you'll tame your layouts—galleries, forms, videos—ensuring sizes stay predictable and your HTML5 pages look pro. Let's size it right!

The Default Problem

By default, CSS uses box-sizing: content-box:

- width and height = content only.

- Padding and border *add* to it—e.g., width: 200px; padding: 20px; border: 5px solid; = 250px total (200 + 20 + 20 + 5 + 5).

Test it:

```
div {
    width: 200px;
    height: 100px;
    padding: 20px;
    border: 5px solid #4682B4;
    background-color: #F0F8FF;
}
```

Check in your browser (Chapter 5)—it's 250px wide, 150px tall—not 200x100px! Chaos for layouts like <form> (Chapter 22).

box-sizing: border-box

Switch to border-box:

- width and height include padding and border—total stays put.

- Same CSS with box-sizing: border-box; = exactly 200x100px— padding and border eat *inside*.

Universal Fix

Apply globally:

```
* {
    box-sizing: border-box;
}
div {
    width: 200px;
    height: 100px;
    padding: 20px;
    border: 5px solid #4682B4;
    background-color: #F0F8FF;
}
```

* targets all elements—now <div> is 200x100px, content shrinks to fit (150x50px inside). Predictable bliss!

Practical Example

Fix your gallery (Chapter 32):

```
<main>
    <h1>My Photos</h1>
    <section class="gallery">
```

```
            <figure>
                <img src="images/pic1.jpg" alt="Pic 1" width="200">
                <figcaption>Summer</figcaption>
            </figure>
        </section>
    </main>
```

CSS:

```css
* {
    box-sizing: border-box;
}
.gallery {
    width: 600px;
    padding: 20px;
    border: 2px solid #FF69B4;
    background-image: linear-gradient(to right, #E6E6FA, #FFF); /*
Chapter 42 */
}
figure {
    width: 200px;
    padding: 15px;
    border: 1px dashed #20B2AA;
    margin: 10px;
}
```

Test it—<gallery> stays 600px wide, <figure> 200px, no overflow—sizes lock in, despite padding and borders!

Why It's Crucial

- **Consistency**: <img> (Chapter 19) at 200px stays 200px—e.g., gallery thumbs.

- **Layout**: <form> inputs (Chapter 22) fit—e.g., 300px wide, padded, bordered, still 300px.

- **Sanity**: <video> containers (Chapter 26) don't bloat—e.g., 400px with 20px padding.

- **Responsiveness**: Preps for Flexbox (Chapter 46)—sizes behave.

Hands-On Practice

In "style.css":

- * { box-sizing: border-box; }.

- <main>: width: 500px; padding: 25px; border: 3px solid #FFD700; background-color: #F5F5F5;.

- <h1>: margin: 0 0 15px; padding: 10px; border-bottom: 2px solid #32CD32;.

- <p>: width: 300px; padding: 20px; border: 1px solid #FF4500;

background-color: #FFF0F5;.

Add to "index.html":

```
<main>
    <h1>Box Sizing</h1>
    <p>This fits perfectly!</p>
</main>
```

Test in your browser—measure with DevTools (right-click > Inspect > Layout). Is <main> 500px? <p> 300px? Add comments—<!-- Box sizing fix -->. Play: remove box-sizing, see bloat, restore it—feel the control!

Tips

- **Global**: * { box-sizing: border-box; }—industry standard, reset chaos.

- **Inheritance**: Kids inherit—<main> sets it, <p> follows.

- **Debug**: Add border to see boxes—1px solid red reveals truth.

- **Test**: Resize—layouts hold tight.

Chapter 46
Centering Elements

Your HTML5 pages are taking shape—text styled, backgrounds glowing, boxes sized perfectly with box-sizing (Chapter 44). But everything's still hugging the left or top, looking a bit lopsided. Centering elements—horizontally, vertically, or both—is a CSS superpower that polishes your layouts, making <h1> headings, <form> boxes, or <img> galleries feel balanced and pro. By the end of this chapter, you'll center your content like a design ninja, using tricks from margins to Flexbox, transforming your site's flow. Let's find the middle ground!

Why Center?

Centering isn't just aesthetics—it's usability. A centered <h1> (Chapter 12) grabs attention, a centered <form> (Chapter 22) feels inviting, a centered <figure> (Chapter 18) in your gallery (Chapter 32) looks deliberate. CSS offers multiple ways—each fits different needs.

Method 1: margin: auto (Horizontal)

- **What**: Centers block elements (e.g., <div>, <p>) horizontally.

- **How**: Set width and margin-left: auto; margin-right: auto;.

```css
.box {

    width: 300px;

    margin: 0 auto;

    background-color: #F0F8FF; /* Alice blue */

    padding: 20px; /* Chapter 43 */

    border: 1px solid #4682B4;

}
```

HTML:

```
<div class="box">Centered!</div>
```

Test it (Chapter 5)—<div> sits dead center, 300px wide, margins push it evenly.

Method 2: text-align (Inline/Text)

- **What**: Centers inline or inline-block content (e.g., <span>, <a>).

- **How**: Parent gets text-align: center;.

Example:

```
h1 {
    text-align: center; /* Chapter 38 */
    color: #FF4500; /* Chapter 40 */
}
nav {
    text-align: center;
}
a {
    display: inline-block; /* Default inline */
    margin: 0 10px;
}
```

HTML:

```
<h1>My Site</h1>
<nav>
    <a href="#">Home</a>
    <a href="#">About</a>
</nav>
```

<h1> and <nav> links center—clean header!

Method 3: Flexbox (Both Ways)

- **What**: Centers anything—horizontal, vertical—using display: flex (Chapter 46 teaser).

- **How**: justify-content: center; (horizontal), align-items: center; (vertical).

Example:

```css
.container {
    display: flex;
    justify-content: center;
    align-items: center;
    height: 200px; /* Needs height for vertical */
    background-color: #E6E6FA; /* Lavender */
}
```

HTML:

```html
<div class="container">
    <p>Right in the middle!</p>
</div>
```

Practical Example

Center your gallery (Chapter 32):

```
<
main>
    <h1>My Photos</h1>
    <section class="gallery">
        <figure>
            <img src="images/pic1.jpg" alt="Pic 1" width="200">
            <figcaption>Summer</figcaption>
        </figure>
    </section>
</main>
```

CSS:

```
* {
    box-sizing: border-box; /* Chapter 44 */
}
h1 {
    text-align: center;
    color: #8A2BE2; /* Chapter 40 */
    margin-bottom: 20px; /* Chapter 43 */
}
.gallery {
    width: 600px;
    margin: 0 auto;
    padding: 20px;
    border: 1px solid #FF69B4;
    background-image: linear-gradient(to right, #E6E6FA, #FFF);
/* Chapter 42 */
}
figure {
    display: flex;
```

```
    justify-content: center;

    align-items: center;

    flex-direction: column;

    background-color: #F5F5F5;

}
```

Test it—<h1> centers text, <gallery> centers block, <figure> centers image and caption vertically—balanced beauty!

Why Centering Matters

- **Focus**: <h1> or <button> (Chapter 25) in the middle grabs eyes.

- **Harmony**: <form> (Chapter 22) centered feels welcoming.

- **Polish**: <video> (Chapter 26) or <img> (Chapter 17) centered looks intentional.

- **Flexibility**: Flexbox adapts—teaser for responsiveness (Chapter 47).

Hands-On Practice

In "style.css":

- <main>: width: 500px; margin: 0 auto; padding: 25px; background-color: #F0FFF0; border: 2px solid #32CD32;.

- <h1>: text-align: center; color: #FF4500; margin-bottom: 15px;.

- .center-box { display: flex; justify-content: center; align-items: center; height: 150px; background-color: #E0FFFF; }.

Add to "index.html":

```
<main>
    <h1>Centered World</h1>
    <div class="center-box">
        <p>I'm perfectly centered!</p>
    </div>
</main>
```

Test in your browser—resize, zoom, check mobile. Does <main> sit middle? <p> flex center? Add comments (Chapter 10)—<!-- Centering styles -->. Play: try text-align: center; on <nav> (Chapter 15), margin: auto; on <figure>, flex <section>—find your center!

Tips

- **Width**: margin: auto needs it—unset = full width, no center.

- **Height**: Flex vertical needs parent height—e.g., 200px.

- **Debug**: Add border: 1px solid red;—see the box.

- **Combine**: Mix methods—<h1> text, <div> block.

What's Next

Centered elements anchor your layout—next, Flexbox (Chapter 47) makes them responsive, refining your <gallery>, <form>, and more!

Chapter 47
Creating Responsive Layouts with Flexbox

Flexbox introduced flexible rows and columns (Chapter 46)—now let's make them dance across screens, from phones to desktops. Responsive layouts with Flexbox use properties like flex-wrap, flex-grow, and media queries (teaser for Chapter 51) to adapt your HTML5 content—galleries, forms, videos—to any viewport. By the end, you'll craft layouts that flex and flow, ensuring your site looks great everywhere. Let's stretch your skills!

Flexbox Recap

- display: flex—parent controls kids.

- flex-direction—row or column.

- justify-content, align-items—space and align.

Responsive Additions

- **flex-wrap**: wrap—items break to new lines if cramped; nowrap (default)—stays single.

- **flex-grow**: Kids grow to fill space—0 (default), 1 (grow equal).

- **flex**: Shorthand—e.g., flex: 1; (grow), flex: 0 0 200px; (fixed).

Basic Responsive Flex

```
.gallery {
    display: flex;
    flex-wrap: wrap;
    justify-content: space-around;
    gap: 20px; /* Modern spacing */
}
figure {
    width: 200px;
```

```
    padding: 15px;

    background-color: #F5F5F5;

    border: 1px solid #20B2AA; /* Chapter 43 */

}
```

HTML:

```
<section class="gallery">

    <figure><img src="images/pic1.jpg" alt="Pic 1" width="200"><-
figcaption>One</figcaption></figure>

    <figure><img src="images/pic2.jpg" alt="Pic 2" width="200"><-
figcaption>Two</figcaption></figure>

    <figure><img src="images/pic3.jpg" alt="Pic 3" width="200"><-
figcaption>Three</figcaption></figure>

</section>
```

Test it—<figure>s line up, wrap on smaller screens—gallery flows (Chapter 32)!

Advanced Flex

- **Grow**: figure { flex-grow: 1; width: 150px; }—each takes equal space, min 150px.

- **Fixed + Grow**: One fixed, others stretch:

```
.sidebar { width: 200px; flex: 0 0 200px; }

.content { flex: 1; }
```

Full Example

For your form (Chapter 22):

```
<main>

    <h1>Contact Me</h1>

    <form class="flex-form">

        <label for="name">Name:</label>
```

```
        <input type="text" id="name" name="name">
        <label for="email">Email:</label>
        <input type="email" id="email" name="email">
        <button type="submit">Send</button>
    </form>
</main>
```

CSS:

```css
* {
    box-sizing: border-box; /* Chapter 44 */
}
main {
    width: 600px;
    margin: 0 auto; /* Chapter 45 */
    padding: 20px;
    background-color: #F0FFF0;
}
.flex-form {
    display: flex;
    flex-wrap: wrap;
    justify-content: space-between;
    gap: 15px;
    background-image: linear-gradient(to right, #E6E6FA, #FFF);
/* Chapter 42 */
}
label, input, button {
    flex: 1 1 200px; /* Grow, shrink, base 200px */
    padding: 10px;
}
button {
    flex: 0 0 100px; /* Fixed */
    background-color: #FF69B4; /* Chapter 41 */
```

```
        color: white;
    }
```

Test it—form items spread, wrap on narrow screens—responsive and sleek!

Why It's Responsive

- **Wrap**: Adapts—e.g., <gallery> fits phones (Chapter 20's mobile hint).

- **Grow**: Fills space—e.g., <nav> links (Chapter 15).

- **Control**: <form> inputs adjust—e.g., <video> rows (Chapter 26).

- **Future**: Preps for media queries—dynamic shifts.

Hands-On Practice

In "style.css":

- .container { display: flex; flex-wrap: wrap; justify-content: space-around; gap: 10px; background-color: #E0FFFF; padding: 20px; }.

- .item { flex: 1 1 150px; padding: 15px; border: 1px solid #32CD32; background-color: #FFF0F5; }.

Add to "index.html":

```
<div class="container">

    <div class="item">A</div>

    <div class="item">B</div>

    <div class="item">C</div>

</div>
```

Test—resize, zoom, check mobile. Do items wrap? Grow evenly? Add comments—<!-- Responsive flex -->. Play: set flex-direction: column; on narrow, flex: 0 0 100px; on one—tweak flow!

Tips

- [ ] **Gap**: Cleaner than margins—modern flex.

- [ ] **Min-Width**: flex: 1 1 200px;—stops squish.

- [ ] **Test**: Shrink to 320px—phone check.

What's Next

Flexbox flows responsively—next, Grid (Chapter 48) adds 2D precision for your <gallery>, <form>, and more!

Chapter 48
Introduction to CSS Grid

Flexbox bends your layouts into responsive rows and columns—now CSS Grid takes it to two dimensions, giving you rows *and* columns with pinpoint control. Perfect for complex layouts—think full-page designs with <header>, <main>, and <footer> (Chapter 11), or grid-based galleries (Chapter 32). By the end, you'll wield display: grid to structure your HTML5 content like a pro architect, setting the stage for responsive mastery. Let's grid it out!

What's CSS Grid?

Grid turns a container into a table-like layout—rows and columns you define. Unlike Flexbox's one-axis flow, Grid controls both:

- **Parent**: display: grid—sets the framework.

- **Children**: Slot into cells—precise placement.

Basic Grid

```css
.grid {
    display: grid;
    grid-template-columns: 200px 200px; /* Two columns */
    grid-gap: 20px; /* Spacing */
}
.item {
    padding: 15px;
    background-color: #F5F5F5;
    border: 1px solid #20B2AA;
}
```

HTML:

```
<div class="grid">
    <div class="item">1</div>
    <div class="item">2</div>
    <div class="item">3</div>
</div>
```

Test it—two columns, items stack and wrap—simple grid power!

Key Properties

- **grid-template-columns**: Sizes—200px 1fr (fixed + fraction).

- **grid-template-rows**: Row heights—100px 200px.

- **grid-gap**: gap shorthand—20px (rows/columns).

Practical Example

Grid your gallery (Chapter 32):

```
<main>
    <h1>My Photos</h1>
    <section class="gallery">
        <figure><img src="images/pic1.jpg" alt="Pic 1"
width="200"><figcaption>One</figcaption></figure>
```

```
            <figure><img src="images/pic2.jpg" alt="Pic 2"
width="200"><figcaption>Two</figcaption></figure>

            <figure><img src="images/pic3.jpg" alt="Pic 3"
width="200"><figcaption>Three</figcaption></figure>

        </section>

    </main>
```

CSS:

```
* {
    box-sizing: border-box; /* Chapter 44 */
}
main {
    width: 800px;
    margin: 0 auto; /* Chapter 45 */
    padding: 20px;
    background-color: #F0FFF0;
}
.gallery {
    display: grid;
    grid-template-columns: repeat(3, 1fr); /* 3 equal */
    grid-gap: 15px;
    background-image: linear-gradient(to right, #E6E6FA, #FFF);
/* Chapter 42 */
}
figure {
    padding: 10px;
    border: 1px solid #FF69B4;
    background-color: #FFF0F5;
}
```

Test it—three-column grid, equal widths, gaps—gallery snaps into place!

Why Grid Rocks

- **2D**: Rows + columns—e.g., <form> + sidebar (Chapter 22).

- **Precision**: Exact cells—e.g., <video> layouts (Chapter 26).

- **Simplicity**: repeat(3, 1fr)—no floats needed.

- **Future**: Preps complex layouts (Chapter 49)—e.g., <header> + <main>.

Hands-On Practice

In "style.css":

- .grid { display: grid; grid-template-columns: 1fr 2fr; grid-gap: 20px; background-color: #E0FFFF; padding: 20px; }.

- .item { padding: 15px; border: 1px solid #32CD32; background-color: #FFF0F5; }.

Add to "index.html":

```
<div class="grid">

    <div class="item">Left</div>

    <div class="item">Right</div>

</div>
```

Test—resize, zoom, check mobile. Does 2fr double 1fr? Add comments—<!-- Grid layout -->. Play: try repeat(2, 200px);, add grid-template-rows: 100px 100px;, test 4 items—build a grid!

Tips

- **Fr**: 1fr = fraction of free space—flexible.

- **Auto**: grid-template-columns: auto 1fr;—content-sized + rest.

- **Debug**: border on items—see cells.

Chapter 49
Building Complex Layouts with Grid

You've dipped into CSS Grid's two-dimensional power (Chapter 48)—now let's crank it up to build complex layouts. Beyond simple rows and columns, Grid's grid-template-areas, grid-template-rows, and named lines let you craft full-page designs—think <header>, <nav>, <main>, and <footer> in one cohesive structure. Perfect for your gallery (Chapter 32), form pages (Chapter 22), or video hubs (Chapter 26), this chapter will turn you into a layout architect by the end, mastering intricate grids for your HTML5 site. Let's construct something epic!

Beyond Basics

- **grid-template-areas**: Names sections—e.g., "header" "main side-bar".

- **grid-template-rows/columns**: Sizes rows/columns—e.g., 100px 1fr.

- **Named Lines**: Label grid lines—e.g., [start] 200px [end]—for placement.

Full-Page Grid

```
.page {
    display: grid;
    grid-template-areas:
        "header header"
        "nav main"
        "footer footer";
    grid-template-rows: 100px 1fr 50px;
    grid-template-columns: 200px 1fr;
    grid-gap: 20px;
}

header { grid-area: header; }
```

```
nav { grid-area: nav; }
main { grid-area: main; }
footer { grid-area: footer; }
```

HTML:

```
<div class="page">
    <header><h1>My Site</h1></header>
    <nav><a href="#">Home</a></nav>
    <main><p>Content here</p></main>
    <footer><p>© 2025</p></footer>
</div>
```

Test it (Chapter 5)—<header> spans top, <nav> left, <main> right, <footer> bottom—structured elegance!

Deep Dive: grid-template-areas

- Dots (.) skip cells—"header header" ". main" "footer footer".

- Multiple rows—define each line in quotes.

- Assign with grid-area—matches HTML to layout.

Named Lines

```
.grid {
    display: grid;
    grid-template-columns: [sidebar-start] 200px [sidebar-end
content-start] 1fr [content-end];
    grid-template-rows: [top] 150px [middle] 1fr [bottom];
    grid-gap: 15px;
}
.sidebar { grid-column: sidebar-start / sidebar-end; }
.content { grid-column: content-start / content-end; grid-row:
middle / bottom; }
```

More control—explicit placement!

Practical Example

Grid your gallery page (Chapter 32):

```html
<main class="layout">
    <header><h1>My Photos</h1></header>
    <nav><a href="#">All</a> <a href="#">Summer</a></nav>
    <section class="gallery">
        <figure><img src="images/pic1.jpg" alt="Pic 1"
width="200"><figcaption>One</figcaption></figure>
        <figure><img src="images/pic2.jpg" alt="Pic 2"
width="200"><figcaption>Two</figcaption></figure>
    </section>
    <footer><p>© 2025</p></footer>
</main>
```

CSS:

```css
* {
    box-sizing: border-box; /* Chapter 44 */
}
.layout {
    display: grid;
    grid-template-areas:
        "header header"
        "nav gallery"
        "footer footer";
    grid-template-rows: 80px 1fr 50px;
    grid-template-columns: 150px 1fr;
    grid-gap: 15px;
    margin: 20px; /* Chapter 43 */
    background-color: #F0FFF0;
}
header {
```

```css
        grid-area: header;

    background-image: linear-gradient(to right, #8A2BE2,
#FF69B4); /* Chapter 42 */

    color: white;

    padding: 10px;

    text-align: center; /* Chapter 38 */
}
nav {

    grid-area: nav;

    padding: 10px;

    border: 1px solid #20B2AA;
}
.gallery {

    grid-area: gallery;

    display: grid; /* Nested grid! */

    grid-template-columns: repeat(auto-fit, minmax(200px, 1fr));

    gap: 10px;

    padding: 15px;
}
footer {

    grid-area: footer;

    background-color: #4682B4;

    color: white;

    text-align: center;
}
figure {

    background-color: #FFF0F5;
}
```

Test it—full layout with nested gallery grid—<header> spans, <nav>
sides, <gallery> adapts—pro-level!

Why Complex Grids Rule

- **Structure**: Full pages—e.g., <form> + sidebar (Chapter 22).

- **Flexibility**: Nested grids—e.g., <video> rows (Chapter 26).

- **Precision**: Areas place—e.g., <h1> + <nav> (Chapter 11).

- **Future**: Responsive next (Chapter 50)—grids scale.

Hands-On Practice

In "style.css":

- .layout { display: grid; grid-template-areas: "top top" "side main" "bottom bottom"; grid-template-rows: 100px 1fr 60px; grid-template-columns: 200px 1fr; grid-gap: 20px; background-color: #E0FFFF; }.

- header { grid-area: top; background-color: #FF4500; }, aside { grid-area: side; border: 1px solid #32CD32; }, etc.

Add to "index.html":

```
<div class="layout">
    <header><h1>Grid Test</h1></header>
    <aside><p>Sidebar</p></aside>
    <main><p>Main content</p></main>
    <footer><p>End</p></footer>
</div>
```

Test—resize, zoom, check mobile. Does it grid? Add comments (Chapter 10)—<!-- Complex grid -->. Play: adjust rows to 50px auto 50px, add a nested grid—build big!

Tips

- **Auto-Fit**: repeat(auto-fit, minmax(200px, 1fr))—responsive columns.

- **Debug**: border on kids—see cells.

- **Names**: Keep grid-area unique—match CSS/HTML.

What's Next

Complex grids frame your site—next, responsive design (Chapter 50) ensures it fits all screens!

Chapter 50
What is Responsive Design?

Your grids and Flexbox layouts shine (Chapters 47-49)—but what happens on a phone? A 600px-wide <gallery> overflows, <form> inputs squash—ouch. Responsive design makes your HTML5 site adapt to any screen—desktop, tablet, phone—using fluid layouts, flexible images, and smart tweaks. By the end, you'll grasp why responsiveness matters for your galleries, forms, and videos, setting up tools like media queries (Chapter 51). Let's make your web stretch!

What's Responsive Design?

Responsive design = one site, all devices. No separate mobile pages—just CSS that adjusts:

- **Fluid Layouts**: Percentages, not pixels—e.g., width: 50%.

- **Flexible Images**: Scale—e.g., max-width: 100% (Chapter 20's srcset).

- **Media Queries**: Rules change by screen—teaser for next chapter.

Why It's Essential

- **Users**: Half browse on phones—<video> (Chapter 26) must fit 320px.

- **SEO**: Google loves mobile-friendly—rank up.

- **Future**: Tablets, watches—your <gallery> (Chapter 32) adapts.

- **Experience**: <form> (Chapter 22) usable on tiny screens.

Principles

- **Relative Units**: %, vw (viewport width)—not px (Chapter 53 teaser).

- **Breakpoints**: Adjust at sizes—e.g., 600px phone, 1200px desktop.

- **Content First**: <h1> (Chapter 12) leads—layout serves it.

Example Prep

```
<main>
    <h1>My Site</h1>
    <section class="content">
        <p>Welcome to my responsive world!</p>
        <img src="images/pic1.jpg" alt="Pic 1">
    </section>
</main>
```

CSS:

```css
* {
    box-sizing: border-box; /* Chapter 44 */
}
main {
    width: 90%;
    margin: 0 auto; /* Chapter 45 */
    padding: 20px;
}
h1 {
    text-align: center; /* Chapter 38 */
    color: #FF4500; /* Chapter 40 */
}
.content {
    background-color: #F0FFF0;
}
img {
    max-width: 100%;
    height: auto;
}
```

Test it—resize to 320px—<main> shrinks to 90%, <img> scales—responsive start!

Why It Ties In

- **Flexbox**: flex-wrap (Chapter 47)—e.g., <gallery> flows.

- **Grid**: auto-fit (Chapter 49)—e.g., <section> adjusts.

- **Images**: srcset (Chapter 20)—e.g., <video> posters (Chapter 29).

- **Forms**: <input> spacing (Chapter 22)—mobile-ready.

Hands-On Practice

In "style.css":

- <main>: width: 95%; margin: 0 auto; padding: 15px; background-color: #E0FFFF;.

- <h1>: text-align: center; color: #4682B4;.

- .box { width: 100%; max-width: 600px; padding: 20px; background-color: #FFF0F5; }.

Add to "index.html":

```
<main>
    <h1>Responsive Test</h1>
    <div class="box">
        <p>This scales!</p>
        <img src="images/pic1.jpg" alt="Pic 1">
    </div>
</main>
```

Test—resize from 1200px to 320px. Does <main> fit? <img> scale? Add comments—<!-- Responsive base -->. Play: set <p> to width: 80%;, test max-width: 400px;—feel the flow!

Tips

- **Mobile**: Test 320px—phone baseline.

- **Images**: max-width: 100%—no overflow.

- **Why**: Prep for media queries—dynamic next!

What's Next

Responsive design sets the goal—media queries (Chapter 51) make it happen for your <gallery>, <form>, and more!

Chapter 51
Media Queries

Responsive design promises adaptability (Chapter 50)—media queries deliver it. With @media, CSS adjusts styles based on screen size, orientation, or device traits, ensuring your HTML5 site—galleries, forms, videos—looks ace on phones, tablets, or desktops. By the end, you'll wield media queries to tweak your layouts, making <h1> shrink, <img> resize, and <form> reflow. Let's query the screen!

What's a Media Query?

A media query is a CSS rule that activates at conditions—e.g., max-width: 600px (phones).

- **Syntax**: @media (condition) { styles }.

- **Conditions**: max-width, min-width, orientation: portrait.

Basic Query

```
h1 {
    font-size: 32px; /* Chapter 37 */
    color: #FF4500; /* Chapter 40 */
}
@media (max-width: 600px) {
    h1 {
        font-size: 24px;
    }
}
```

HTML:

```
<h1>My Site</h1>
```

Test it—above 600px, <h1> is 32px; below, 24px—phone-friendly!

Breakpoints

Common sizes:

- **320-600px**: Phones—<form> inputs (Chapter 22).

- **600-900px**: Tablets—<gallery> (Chapter 32).

- **1200px+**: Desktops—<video> (Chapter 26).

Full Example

For your gallery:

```
<main>

    <h1>My Photos</h1>

    <section class="gallery">

        <figure><img src="images/pic1.jpg" alt="Pic 1"
width="200"><figcaption>One</figcaption></figure>

        <figure><img src="images/pic2.jpg" alt="Pic 2"
width="200"><figcaption>Two</figcaption></figure>

    </section>

</main>
```

CSS:

```
* {

    box-sizing: border-box; /* Chapter 44 */

}

main {

    width: 90%;

    margin: 0 auto; /* Chapter 45 */

    padding: 20px;

    background-color: #F0FFF0;

}

h1 {

    text-align: center;
```

```css
    font-size: 36px;
    color: #8A2BE2;
}
.gallery {
    display: flex; /* Chapter 47 */
    flex-wrap: wrap;
    gap: 15px;
    justify-content: space-around;
}
figure {
    flex: 1 1 200px;
    padding: 10px;
    border: 1px solid #FF69B4;
}
@media (max-width: 600px) {
    h1 {
        font-size: 24px;
    }
    .gallery {
        flex-direction: column;
        align-items: center;
    }
    figure {
        width: 100%;
        max-width: 300px;
    }
}
```

On computer:

My Photos

On cellphone:

My Photos

Why Media Queries Matter

- **Adapt**: <h1> shrinks—e.g., <video> titles (Chapter 26).

- **Flow**: <gallery> stacks—e.g., phone fit (Chapter 32).

- **Usability**: <form> reflows—e.g., inputs readable (Chapter 22).

- **Modernity**: Mobile-first next (Chapter 52)—future-ready.

Hands-On Practice

In "style.css":

- <main>: width: 95%; margin: 0 auto; padding: 20px; background-color: #E0FFFF;.

- .grid { display: grid; grid-template-columns: repeat(2, 1fr); gap: 20px; } (Chapter 48).

- @media (max-width: 768px) { .grid { grid-template-columns: 1fr; } h1 { font-size: 20px; } }.

Add to "index.html":

```
<main>
    <h1>Media Test</h1>
    <div class="grid">
        <p>Column 1</p>
        <p>Column 2</p>
    </div>
</main>
```

Test—resize from 1200px to 320px. Does grid stack? <h1> shrink? Add comments—<!-- Media query -->. Play: add @media (min-width: 900px) for big screens—tweak styles!

Tips

- **Max/Min**: max-width—smaller; min-width—larger.

- **Test**: DevTools (Responsive mode)—320px, 768px.

- **Combine**: Flex + Grid + Queries—power trio.

Chapter 52
Mobile-First Design Approach

You've got media queries adapting your layouts (Chapter 51)—but what if you flipped the script? Mobile-first design starts with small screens (e.g., phones at 320px) and scales up, not down, using min-width queries. It's a smarter way to ensure your HTML5 site—galleries, forms, videos—shines on mobiles (half the web's traffic) before desktops. By the end, you'll build from a mobile base, making your <h1>, <img>, and <form> responsive from the ground up. Let's shrink to grow!

What's Mobile-First?

Traditional design (desktop-first) uses max-width—style big, tweak small. Mobile-first reverses it:

- **Base**: Style for phones—minimal, fast.

- **Enhance**: Add for larger screens with min-width.

- **Why**: Mobile's king—<video> (Chapter 26) must load quick, <gallery> (Chapter 32) fit tight.

How It Works

- Start with mobile CSS—e.g., font-size: 16px for <h1>.

- Add @media (min-width: 768px)—e.g., font-size: 24px for tablets+.

Basic Example

```
h1 {
    font-size: 18px; /* Mobile base */
    text-align: center; /* Chapter 38 */
    color: #FF4500; /* Chapter 40 */
}
p {
    font-size: 14px;
```

```
        padding: 10px; /* Chapter 43 */
}
@media (min-width: 768px) {
    h1 {
        font-size: 28px;
    }
    p {
        font-size: 16px;
    }
}
```

HTML:

```
<h1>My Site</h1>
<p>Welcome to mobile-first!</p>
```

Test it (Chapter 5)—below 768px (phone), smaller text; above (tablet/ desktop), it grows—mobile-first flow!

Full Mobile-First Layout

For your gallery (Chapter 32):

```
<main>
    <h1>My Photos</h1>
    <section class="gallery">
        <figure><img src="images/pic1.jpg" alt="Pic 1"><figcap-
tion>One</figcaption></figure>
        <figure><img src="images/pic2.jpg" alt="Pic 2"><figcap-
tion>Two</figcaption></figure>
    </section>
</main>
```

CSS:

```css
* {
    box-sizing: border-box; /* Chapter 44 */
}
main {
    width: 100%;
    padding: 15px;
    background-color: #F0FFF0;
}
h1 {
    font-size: 20px;
    text-align: center;
    color: #8A2BE2;
    margin-bottom: 10px;
}
.gallery {
    display: flex; /* Chapter 47 */
    flex-direction: column;
    gap: 10px;
}
figure {
    padding: 10px;
    border: 1px solid #FF69B4;
    background-color: #FFF0F5;
}
img {
    max-width: 100%; /* Chapter 17 */
    height: auto;
}
@media (min-width: 600px) {
    main {
        width: 90%;
```

```
        margin: 0 auto; /* Chapter 45 */
    }
    h1 {
        font-size: 30px;
    }
    .gallery {
        flex-direction: row;
        flex-wrap: wrap;
        justify-content: space-around;
    }
    figure {
        flex: 1 1 200px;
    }
}
@media (min-width: 900px) {
    main {
        width: 800px;
    }
    h1 {
        font-size: 36px;
    }
}
```

Test it—phone (320px): stacked, small; tablet (600px): row, medium; desktop (900px): wide, big—mobile-first magic!

Why Mobile-First Wins

- **Speed**: <video> (Chapter 26) light—mobile loads fast.
- **Focus**: <form> (Chapter 22) usable—core first.
- **Scalability**: <gallery> (Chapter 32) grows—enhance, don't shrink.
- **SEO**: Google prioritizes mobile—rank up.

Hands-On Practice

In "style.css":

- <main>: width: 100%; padding: 10px; background-color: #E0FFFF;.

- <h1>: font-size: 16px; text-align: center; color: #4682B4;.

- .flex { display: flex; flex-direction: column; gap: 10px; }.

- @media (min-width: 768px) { main { width: 80%; margin: 0 auto; } h1 { font-size: 24px; } .flex { flex-direction: row; justify-content: center; } }.

Add to "index.html":

```
<main>
    <h1>Mobile First</h1>
    <div class="flex">
        <p>A</p>
        <p>B</p>
    </div>
</main>
```

Test—resize from 320px to 1200px. Does it stack, then row? Add comments (Chapter 10)—<!-- Mobile-first -->. Play: add @media (min-width: 1000px)—bigger <h1>—scale up!

Tips

- **Base**: Keep mobile lean—<img> scales (Chapter 20).

- **Breakpoints**: 600px, 768px, 1200px—test each.

- **Tools**: DevTools Responsive mode—320px start.

What's Next

Mobile-first sets the foundation—relative units (Chapter 53) make it fluid for your <gallery>, <form>, and more!

Chapter 53
Using Relative Units (em, rem, %, vh, vw)

Mobile-first design adapts your layouts (Chapter 52)—now let's make them fluid with relative units: em, rem, %, vh, and vw. Unlike fixed pixels (px), these scale with context—parent size, root size, or viewport—ensuring your HTML5 site's <h1>, <img>, and <form> flex across devices. By the end, you'll ditch rigid sizes, crafting responsive <gallery> (Chapter 32), <video> (Chapter 26), and more with stretchy precision. Let's get relative!

What Are Relative Units?

- **em**: Relative to parent's font-size—1em = parent's size.

- **rem**: Relative to root (<html>) font-size—1rem = root's size.

- **%**: Percentage of parent's dimension—e.g., width: 50%.

- **vh/vw**: Viewport height/width—1vh = 1% of height, 1vw = 1% of width.

How They Work

- Default: <html> font-size = 16px (browser norm).

- 1em in <p> with parent at 20px = 20px.

- 1rem anywhere = 16px (unless <html> changes).

- 50% width = half parent's width.

CSS:

```
html {
    font-size: 16px; /* Root */
}
h1 {
    font-size: 2rem; /* 32px */
```

```
        margin-bottom: 1em; /* Parent-based */
}
p {
    font-size: 1.2em; /* Parent's size */
    width: 80%;
}
section {
    height: 50vh;
    width: 90vw;
}
}
```

HTML:

```
<section>
    <h1>My Site</h1>
    <p>Welcome!</p>
</section>
```

\<h1\> 32px, \<p\> scales with parent, \<section\> fills viewport—fluid!

Full Responsive Example

For your form (Chapter 22):

```
<main>
    <h1>Contact Me</h1>
    <form class="flex-form">
        <label for="name">Name:</label>
        <input type="text" id="name" name="name">
    </form>
</main>
```

CSS:

```css
* {
    box-sizing: border-box; /* Chapter 44 */
}
html {
    font-size: 16px;
}
main {
    width: 90%;
    margin: 0 auto; /* Chapter 45 */
    padding: 2rem; /* 32px */
    background-color: #F0FFF0;
}
h1 {
    font-size: 1.5rem; /* 24px */
    text-align: center;
    color: #8A2BE2;
    margin-bottom: 1em;
}
.flex-form {
    display: flex;
    flex-direction: column;
    gap: 1rem;
    width: 100%;
    max-width: 500px;
}
label {
    font-size: 1em; /* Parent */
}
input {
    width: 100%;
    padding: 0.5rem;
```

```
      font-size: 1rem;
      border: 1px solid #FF69B4;
  }
@media (min-width: 600px) { /* Chapter 52 */
      h1 {
          font-size: 2rem; /* 32px */
      }
      .flex-form {
          flex-direction: row;
          flex-wrap: wrap;
      }
      label, input {
          flex: 1 1 45%;
      }
  }
```

Test—phone: stacked, small; desktop: row, bigger—relative units flex!

Why Relative Units Matter

- **Fluidity**: <img> % (Chapter 17)—scales—e.g., <gallery>.

- **Consistency**: <rem> roots—e.g., <form> (Chapter 22).

- **Viewport**: <vh> heights—e.g., <video> (Chapter 26).

- **Adapt**: <em> nests—e.g., <figcaption> (Chapter 18).

Hands-On Practice

In "style.css":

- <main>: width: 95vw; padding: 1.5rem; background-color: #E0FFFF;.

- <h1>: font-size: 1.8rem; margin-bottom: 1em; color: #4682B4;.

- .box { width: 80%; height: 20vh; padding: 1rem; font-size: 1.2em; background-color: #FFF0F5; }.

Add to "index.html":

```
<main>

    <h1>Relative Test</h1>

    <div class="box">Fluid content!</div>

</main>
```

Test—resize from 320px to 1200px. Does <main> stretch? <box> fit? Add comments—<!-- Relative units -->. Play: set <html> to font-size: 18px;, use 2em on <p>—scale it!

Tips

- **Root**: Set <html>—16px base.

- **Max**: max-width: 100%;—caps overflow.

- **Test**: Zoom—relative adjusts.

What's Next

Relative units flow—transitions (Chapter 54) add motion to your <gallery>, <form>, and more!

Chapter 54
CSS Transitions

Your layouts flex and scale with relative units (Chapter 53)—now let's animate them! CSS transitions add smooth changes to properties like color, width, or font-size when states shift (e.g., hover). They bring life to your HTML5 site's <a> links, <button> clicks, and <img> hovers—think fading colors or sliding boxes. By the end, you'll transition your <form>, <gallery>, and <video> elements into dynamic delights. Let's move it!

What's a Transition?

A transition animates a property change over time—e.g., color from blue to red in 0.3 seconds.

- **Syntax**: transition: property duration timing-function delay;.

- **Properties**: color, background, width, etc.

Basic Transition

```css
a {
    color: #4682B4; /* Chapter 40 */
    transition: color 0.3s ease;
}
a:hover {
    color: #FF4500;
}
```

HTML:

```html
<a href="#">Hover me</a>
```

Test it—hover, <a> fades from blue to orange—smooth, not jarring!

Key Parts

- **property**: What changes—all for everything.

- **duration**: Seconds (e.g., 0.5s) or milliseconds (500ms).

- **timing-function**: ease (soft), linear (steady), ease-in-out.

- **delay**: Wait—e.g., 0.2s.

Full Example

For your gallery (Chapter 32):

```html
<main>
    <h1>My Photos</h1>
    <section class="gallery">
        <figure>
            <img src="images/pic1.jpg" alt="Pic 1" width="200">
            <figcaption>One</figcaption>
        </figure>
    </section>
</main>
```

CSS:

```css
* {
    box-sizing: border-box; /* Chapter 44 */
}
main {
    width: 90%;
    margin: 0 auto; /* Chapter 45 */
    padding: 1rem; /* Chapter 53 */ .
    background-color: #F0FFF0;
}
h1 {
```

```css
    font-size: 2rem;
    text-align: center;
    color: #8A2BE2;
    transition: color 0.5s ease-in-out;
}
h1:hover {
    color: #FF69B4;
}
.gallery {
    display: flex;
    flex-wrap: wrap;
    gap: 1rem;
}
figure {
    padding: 10px;
    border: 1px solid #20B2AA;
    background-color: #FFF0F5;
    transition: transform 0.3s ease, background-color 0.4s ease;
}
figure:hover {
    transform: scale(1.05); /* Zoom */
    background-color: #E6E6FA;
}
img {
    max-width: 100%;
}
@media (min-width: 600px) { /* Chapter 52 */
    .gallery {
        justify-content: space-around;
    }
}
```

Test—hover \<h1\> fades pink, \<figure\> zooms and shifts color—interactive pop!

Why Transitions Shine

- **Engagement**: <a> (Chapter 15) hovers—click me!

- **Feedback**: <button> (Chapter 25) shifts—pressed feel.

- **Polish**: <img> (Chapter 17) scales—e.g., <gallery> hover.

- **Subtlety**: <video> (Chapter 26) buttons fade—smooth UI.

Hands-On Practice

In "style.css":

- <h1>: font-size: 1.8rem; color: #4682B4; transition: color 0.5s ease;, h1:hover { color: #FF4500; }.

- .box { width: 200px; height: 100px; background-color: #E0FFFF; transition: width 0.4s ease-in, background-color 0.3s linear; }, .box:hover { width: 300px; background-color: #FFF0F5; }.

Add to "index.html":

```
<main>

    <h1>Transition Test</h1>

    <div class="box">Hover me!</div>

</main>
```

Test—hover, watch <h1> fade, <box> stretch. Add comments—<!-- Transitions -->. Play: try transform: rotate(5deg);, opacity: 0.7;—animate wild!

Tips

- **Multiple**: transition: color 0.3s, width 0.5s;.

- **Test**: Hover slow—see timing.

- **Fallback**: Works everywhere—no JS yet.

Chapter 55
Transformations
(Scale, Rotate, Translate, Skew)

You've added smooth transitions to your CSS toolkit (Chapter 54)—now let's twist, stretch, and shift your HTML5 elements with transformations. The transform property scales, rotates, translates (moves), or skews anything from <img> to <div>, bringing flair to your galleries, forms, and videos. Think zooming thumbnails on hover or sliding buttons—by the end, you'll wield transform to make your <h1>, <figure>, and <button> dance, turning static pages into dynamic experiences. Let's transform your web!

What's transform?

transform changes an element's shape or position—2D fun without altering layout flow:

- **scale**: Grows/shrinks—e.g., scale(1.2) (120%).

- **rotate**: Spins—e.g., rotate(45deg) (45 degrees).

- **translate**: Moves—e.g., translate(20px, 10px) (x, y).

- **skew**: Tilts—e.g., skew(10deg) (x-axis slant).

Pair with transition (Chapter 54) for smoothness!

Basic Transformations

```
img {
    transition: transform 0.3s ease;
}
img:hover {
    transform: scale(1.1); /* Zoom 110% */
}
```

HTML:

```
<img src="images/pic1.jpg" alt="Pic 1" width="200">
```

Test it (Chapter 5)—hover, <img> grows gently—eye-catching!

Full Transform Set

- **Scale**: scale(2) (200%), scale(0.5) (50%), scaleX(1.5) (width only).

- **Rotate**: rotate(90deg), rotate(-45deg)—clockwise or counter.

- **Translate**: translate(50px) (x), translate(20px, 30px) (x, y).

- **Skew**: skew(20deg) (x), skew(0, 15deg) (y).

Practical Example

For your gallery (Chapter 32):

```
<main>
    <h1>My Photos</h1>
    <section class="gallery">
        <figure>
            <img src="images/pic1.jpg" alt="Pic 1" width="200">
            <figcaption>One</figcaption>
        </figure>
    </section>
</main>
```

CSS:

```
* {
    box-sizing: border-box; /* Chapter 44 */
}
main {
    width: 90%;
    margin: 0 auto; /* Chapter 45 */
```

```css
    padding: 1rem; /* Chapter 53 */
    background-color: #F0FFF0;
}
h1 {
    font-size: 2rem;
    text-align: center; /* Chapter 38 */
    color: #8A2BE2; /* Chapter 40 */
    transition: transform 0.5s ease;
}
h1:hover {
    transform: rotate(5deg); /* Slight tilt */
}
.gallery {
    display: flex; /* Chapter 47 */
    flex-wrap: wrap;
    gap: 1rem;
}
figure {
    padding: 10px;
    border: 1px solid #FF69B4;
    background-color: #FFF0F5;
    transition: transform 0.4s ease-in-out;
}
figure:hover {
    transform: scale(1.05) translate(0, -10px); /* Zoom + lift */
}
img {
    max-width: 100%;
    transition: transform 0.3s ease;
}
img:hover {
    transform: skew(5deg); /* Subtle slant */
}
```

```
@media (min-width: 600px) { /* Chapter 52 */

    .gallery {

        justify-content: space-around;

    }

}
```

Test it—hover <h1> tilts, <figure> lifts, <img> skews—interactive delight!

Why Transformations Matter

- **Engagement**: <img> zooms—e.g., <gallery> (Chapter 32) hovers.

- **Feedback**: <button> (Chapter 25) shifts—e.g., <form> (Chapter 22).

- **Flair**: <video> (Chapter 26) play button rotates—cool UI.

- **No JS**: Pure CSS—fast, simple.

Hands-On Practice

In "style.css":

- <h1>: font-size: 1.8rem; color: #4682B4; transition: transform 0.5s ease;, h1:hover { transform: rotate(-10deg); }.

- .box { width: 200px; height: 100px; background-color: #E0FFFF; transition: transform 0.3s ease; }, .box:hover { transform: translate(20px, 0) scale(1.2); }.

Add to "index.html":

```
<main>

    <h1>Transform Test</h1>

    <div class="box">Hover me!</div>

</main>
```

Test—hover, <h1> spins, <box> shifts and grows. Add comments (Chapter 10)—<!-- Transforms -->. Play: try skew(15deg), translate(0, -20px)—mix it up!

Tips

- **Combine**: transform: scale(1.1) rotate(10deg);—multi-effect.

- **Origin**: transform-origin: top left;—pivot point.

- **Test**: Slow hover—check smoothness.

What's Next

Transforms twist—keyframes (Chapter 56) animate your <gallery>, <form>, and more!

Chapter 56
Keyframe Animations

→ Starting from this chapter, it is necessary for you to test everything in your browser. The websites will feature transitions and movements.

Transitions morph on trigger (Chapter 54), transformations shape the move (Chapter 55)—now keyframes make your HTML5 elements animate continuously or on demand. With @keyframes and the animation property, you'll create loops, bounces, or fades for your <h1>, <img>, or <button>, adding motion to galleries, forms, and videos. By the end, you'll craft animations that bring your site to life, no JavaScript needed. Let's animate the web!

What's a Keyframe Animation?

- **@keyframes**: Defines steps—e.g., 0% (start), 100% (end).

- **animation**: Applies it—name, duration, timing, etc.

Basic Animation

```
h1 {
    animation: pulse 2s infinite ease-in-out;
}
@keyframes pulse {
    0% { transform: scale(1); }
    50% { transform: scale(1.1); }
    100% { transform: scale(1); }
}
```

HTML:

```
<h1>My Site</h1>
```

Test it—<h1> pulses endlessly—scales up, then back, every 2 seconds!

Animation Properties

- **animation-name**: Links to @keyframes.

- **animation-duration**: 2s, 500ms.

- **animation-iteration-count**: infinite, 3.

- **animation-timing-function**: ease, linear.

- **Shorthand**: animation: pulse 2s infinite ease;.

Full Example

For your gallery (Chapter 32):

```html
<main>
    <h1>My Photos</h1>
    <section class="gallery">
        <figure>
            <img src="images/pic1.jpg" alt="Pic 1" width="200">
            <figcaption>One</figcaption>
        </figure>
    </section>
</main>
```

CSS:

```css
* {
    box-sizing: border-box; /* Chapter 44 */
}
main {
    width: 90%;
    margin: 0 auto; /* Chapter 45 */
    padding: 1rem; /* Chapter 53 */
    background-color: #F0FFF0;
}
```

```css
h1 {
    font-size: 2rem;
    text-align: center;
    color: #8A2BE2;
    animation: fadeIn 1.5s ease-in;
}
.gallery {
    display: flex;
    flex-wrap: wrap;
    gap: 1rem;
}
figure {
    padding: 10px;
    border: 1px solid #FF69B4;
    background-color: #FFF0F5;
    animation: bounce 2s infinite ease-in-out;
}
img {
    max-width: 100%;
}
@keyframes fadeIn {
    0% { opacity: 0; transform: translateY(-20px); }
    100% { opacity: 1; transform: translateY(0); }
}
@keyframes bounce {
    0%, 100% { transform: translateY(0); }
    50% { transform: translateY(-15px); }
}
@media (min-width: 600px) { /* Chapter 52 */
    .gallery {
        justify-content: space-around;
    }
}
```

Test—<h1> fades in, <figure> bounces forever—motion magic!

Why Animations Pop

- **Attention**: <h1> fades—e.g., <video> (Chapter 26) intro.

- **Fun**: <figure> bounces—e.g., <gallery> (Chapter 32).

- **Feedback**: <button> (Chapter 25) pulses—clickable.

- **No JS**: CSS-driven—lightweight.

Hands-On Practice

In "style.css":

- <h1>: font-size: 1.8rem; color: #4682B4; animation: slide 1s ease;, @keyframes slide { 0% { transform: translateX(-100%); } 100% { transform: translateX(0); } }.

- .box { width: 200px; height: 100px; background-color: #E0FFFF; animation: spin 3s infinite linear; }, @keyframes spin { 0% { transform: rotate(0deg); } 100% { transform: rotate(360deg); } }.

Add to "index.html":

```
<main>
    <h1>Animation Test</h1>
    <div class="box">Spin me!</div>
</main>
```

Test—<h1> slides, <box> spins. Add comments—<!-- Keyframes -->. Play: try opacity fade, scale pulse—animate wild!

Tips

- **Steps**: More %—e.g., 25%, 75%.

- **Direction**: animation-direction: alternate;—back-and-forth.

- **Test**: Slow—see each frame.

What's Next

Keyframes animate—<div> (Chapter 57) structures your <gallery>, <form>, and more!

Chapter 57
Understanding the <div> Element

Animations bring motion, but your HTML5 content needs a backbone. The <div> element is that backbone—a generic block container grouping your <h1>, <p>, <img>, or <form> into layout-ready chunks. It's the unsung hero behind your galleries, forms, and videos, paired with CSS (Chapters 34-56) for style and structure. By the end, you'll grasp <div>'s role, setting up <section>-like blocks with flexibility. Let's divide and conquer!

What's a <div>?

- **Block**: Takes full width, stacks vertically—unlike inline <span> (future chapter).

- **Neutral**: No meaning—pure container, unlike <header> (Chapter 11).

- **CSS Buddy**: Styled with width, display, background—e.g., Flexbox (Chapter 47).

Basic Use

```
<div>
    <h1>My Site</h1>
    <p>Welcome!</p>
</div>
```

CSS:

```
div {
    padding: 20px; /* Chapter 43 */
    background-color: #F0FFF0; /* Chapter 41 */
    border: 1px solid #4682B4;
}
```

Test it—<div> wraps, styles as a box—simple grouping!

Practical Example

For your gallery (Chapter 32):

```
<main>
    <div class="header">
        <h1>My Photos</h1>
    </div>
    <div class="gallery">
        <figure>
            <img src="images/pic1.jpg" alt="Pic 1" width="200">
            <figcaption>One</figcaption>
        </figure>
    </div>
</main>
```

CSS:

```
* {
    box-sizing: border-box; /* Chapter 44 */
}
main {
    width: 90%;
    margin: 0 auto; /* Chapter 45 */
    padding: 1rem; /* Chapter 53 */
}
.header {
    background-image: linear-gradient(to right, #8A2BE2,
#FF69B4); /* Chapter 42 */
    padding: 10px;
    text-align: center; /* Chapter 38 */
}
h1 {
```

```css
      font-size: 2rem;
      color: white;
      margin: 0;
}
.gallery {
      display: flex; /* Chapter 47 */
      flex-wrap: wrap;
      gap: 1rem;
      padding: 15px;
      border: 1px solid #20B2AA;
      background-color: #FFF0F5;
      transition: transform 0.3s ease; /* Chapter 54 */
}
.gallery:hover {
      transform: scale(1.02); /* Chapter 55 */
}
@media (min-width: 600px) { /* Chapter 52 */
      .gallery {
            justify-content: space-around;
      }
}
```

Test—<div.header> frames <h1>, <div.gallery> groups <figure>—structured and styled!

Why <div> Matters

- **Group**: Wraps—e.g., <form> (Chapter 22) sections.
- **Layout**: Flex/Grid base—e.g., <gallery> (Chapter 32).
- **Style**: <video> (Chapter 26) containers—e.g., background.
- **Flexibility**: No semantics—molds to need.

Hands-On Practice

In "style.css":

- .wrapper { width: 95%; margin: 0 auto; padding: 1.5rem; background-color: #E0FFFF; }.

- .top { background-color: #FF4500; padding: 10px; text-align: center; }.

- .content { display: grid; grid-template-columns: 1fr; gap: 10px; border: 1px solid #32CD32; } (Chapter 48).

Add to "index.html":

```
<div class="wrapper">
    <div class="top"><h1>Div Test</h1></div>
    <div class="content">
        <p>Part 1</p>
        <p>Part 2</p>
    </div>
</div>
```

Test—resize, zoom, check mobile. Does <wrapper> hold? <content> grid? Add comments—<!-- Div structure -->. Play: add transform: rotate(2deg); on hover—shape it!

Tips

- **Class**: <div class="x">—target with CSS (Chapter 36).

- **Nesting**: <div> in <div>—layer deep.

- **Debug**: border—see boxes.

Chapter 58
Grouping Content with <div>

You've met the <div> element as a versatile block container (Chapter 57)—now let's harness its power to group your HTML5 content into logical, layout-ready chunks. Whether it's wrapping a <form> section, organizing a <gallery>, or framing a <video> player, <div> with CSS turns chaos into order. By the end, you'll use <div> to structure your pages like a pro, setting up your <h1>, <p>, and <img> for styling and responsiveness. Let's group it up!

Why Group with <div>?

- **Structure**: <div> bundles—e.g., <nav> + <h1> (Chapter 11).

- **Layout**: Flexbox (Chapter 47) or Grid (Chapter 48) needs a parent—<div> fits.

- **Style**: Apply one CSS rule—e.g., <gallery> (Chapter 32) background.

- **Clarity**: Nesting separates—e.g., <form> (Chapter 22) parts.

Basic Grouping

```
<div class="intro">

    <h1>Welcome</h1>

    <p>This is my site.</p>

</div>
```

CSS:

```
.intro {

    padding: 20px; /* Chapter 43 */

    background-color: #F0FFF0; /* Chapter 41 */
```

```
    border: 1px solid #4682B4;
}
```

Test it (Chapter 5)—<div> groups <h1> and <p> into a styled box—neat and tidy!

Nested Grouping

```
<div class="container">
    <div class="header">
        <h1>My Site</h1>
    </div>
    <div class="content">
        <p>Here's some info.</p>
        <img src="images/pic1.jpg" alt="Pic 1" width="200">
    </div>
</div>
```

CSS:

```
.container {
    width: 90%; /* Chapter 52 */
    margin: 0 auto; /* Chapter 45 */
    padding: 1rem; /* Chapter 53 */
}
.header {
    background-image: linear-gradient(to right, #8A2BE2, #FF69B4); /*
Chapter 42 */
    color: white;
    padding: 10px;
    text-align: center; /* Chapter 38 */
}
.content {
    padding: 15px;
    border: 1px solid #20B2AA;
```

```
    background-color: #FFF0F5;
}
```

Test—<container> wraps, <header> crowns, <content> holds—layered structure!

Practical Example

For your gallery (Chapter 32):

```
<main>
    <div class="top-section">
        <h1>My Photos</h1>
        <p>A collection of moments.</p>
    </div>
    <div class="gallery-wrapper">
        <div class="gallery">
            <figure>
                <img src="images/pic1.jpg" alt="Pic 1"
width="200">
                <figcaption>One</figcaption>
            </figure>
            <figure>
                <img src="images/pic2.jpg" alt="Pic 2"
width="200">
                <figcaption>Two</figcaption>
            </figure>
        </div>
    </div>
</main>
```

CSS:

```
* {
    box-sizing: border-box; /* Chapter 44 */
}
```

```css
main {
    width: 95%;
    margin: 0 auto;
    padding: 1.5rem;
    background-color: #F0FFF0;
}
.top-section {
    padding: 20px;
    background-color: #E6E6FA;
    text-align: center;
    border-bottom: 2px solid #FF69B4;
}
h1 {
    font-size: 2rem; /* Chapter 53 */
    color: #8A2BE2;
    margin: 0 0 10px;
}
p {
    font-size: 1rem;
    color: #4682B4;
}
.gallery-wrapper {
    padding: 15px;
    background-image: linear-gradient(to bottom, #FFF, #E0FFFF);
}
.gallery {
    display: flex; /* Chapter 47 */
    flex-wrap: wrap;
    gap: 1rem;
    transition: transform 0.3s ease; /* Chapter 54 */
}
.gallery:hover {
    transform: scale(1.02); /* Chapter 55 */
```

```
  }
figure {

    padding: 10px;

    border: 1px solid #20B2AA;

    background-color: #FFF0F5;

}

@media (min-width: 600px) { /* Chapter 52 */

    .gallery {

        justify-content: space-around;

    }

}
```

Test—<top-section> intros, <gallery-wrapper> frames <gallery>—grouped and gorgeous!

Why Grouping Matters

- **Order**: <form> (Chapter 22) splits—e.g., labels vs. inputs.

- **Layout**: <gallery> (Chapter 32) nests—e.g., Flexbox parent.

- **Style**: <video> (Chapter 26) container—e.g., gradient backdrop.

- **Scale**: Preps responsiveness—e.g., <main> adjusts.

Hands-On Practice

In "style.css":

- .wrapper { width: 90%; margin: 0 auto; padding: 1rem; background-color: #E0FFFF; }.

- .title-box { padding: 15px; background-color: #FF4500; color: white; text-align: center; }.

- .content-box { padding: 20px; border: 1px solid #32CD32; background-color: #FFF0F5; display: grid; grid-template-columns: 1fr; gap: 10px; } (Chapter 48).

Add to "index.html":

```
<main>

    <div class="wrapper">
```

```
        <div class="title-box">
            <h1>Group Test</h1>
        </div>
        <div class="content-box">
            <p>Section 1</p>
            <p>Section 2</p>
        </div>
    </div>
</main>
```

Test—resize, zoom, check mobile. Does <wrapper> unify? <content-box> grid? Add comments (Chapter 10)—<!-- Div grouping -->. Play: nest another <div> in <content-box>, add flex—layer it!

Tips

- **Class**: <div class="x">—target precisely (Chapter 36).

- **Nesting**: Deep layers—<div> in <div> in <div>.

- **Debug**: border: 1px solid red;—see boxes.

What's Next

Grouped <div>s organize—styling them (Chapter 59) polishes your <gallery>, <form>, and more!

Chapter 59
Styling <div> Elements

Your <div>s are grouping content like champs (Chapter 58)—now let's make them shine with CSS. Styling <div> elements with properties like background, border, padding, and transform turns plain containers into standout blocks for your HTML5 site's forms, galleries, and videos. By the end, you'll dress up your <div>s, enhancing <h1>, <img>, and <form> layouts with visual flair and structure. Let's style those boxes!

Why Style <div>?

- **Visuals**: <div> backgrounds—e.g., <gallery> (Chapter 32) texture.

- **Borders**: Define—e.g., <form> (Chapter 22) sections.

- **Space**: Padding/margin—e.g., <video> (Chapter 26) breathing room.

- **Motion**: Transitions—e.g., <div> hovers (Chapter 54).

Basic Styling

```
.content {
    background-color: #F0FFF0; /* Chapter 41 */
    padding: 20px; /* Chapter 43 */
    border: 1px solid #4682B4;
    width: 90%; /* Chapter 52 */
    margin: 0 auto; /* Chapter 45 */
}
```

HTML:

```
<div class="content">
    <p>Styled div!</p>
</div>
```

Test—<div> glows green, padded, bordered, centered—styled simplicity!

Advanced Styling

```css
.header {
    background-image: linear-gradient(to right, #8A2BE2,
#FF69B4); /* Chapter 42 */

    color: white;

    padding: 15px;

    border-bottom: 2px dashed #FF4500;

    text-align: center; /* Chapter 38 */

    transition: transform 0.3s ease; /* Chapter 54 */
}
.header:hover {

    transform: scale(1.05); /* Chapter 55 */

}
```

Test with <div class="header"><h1>Hi</h1></div>—gradient, dashed, zooms—fancy!

Practical Example

For your form (Chapter 22):

```html
<main>
    <div class="form-header">
        <h1>Contact Me</h1>
    </div>
    <div class="form-body">
        <form>
            <label for="name">Name:</label>
            <input type="text" id="name" name="name">
        </form>
    </div>
</main>
```

CSS:

```css
* {
    box-sizing: border-box; /* Chapter 44 */
}
main {
    width: 95%;
    margin: 0 auto;
    padding: 1.5rem; /* Chapter 53 */
    background-color: #F0FFF0;
}
.form-header {
    background-color: #E6E6FA;
    padding: 20px;
    border: 1px solid #8A2BE2;
    text-align: center;
    animation: fadeIn 1s ease-in; /* Chapter 56 */
}
@keyframes fadeIn {
    0% { opacity: 0; }
    100% { opacity: 1; }
}
h1 {
    font-size: 2rem;
    color: #8A2BE2;
    margin: 0;
}
.form-body {
    padding: 25px;
    border: 2px solid #FF69B4;
    background-image: linear-gradient(to bottom, #FFF, #E0FFFF);
    transition: box-shadow 0.3s ease;
}
```

```css
.form-body:hover {
    box-shadow: 0 4px 8px rgba(0, 0, 0, 0.2); /* Shadow */
}
label {
    display: block;
    margin-bottom: 0.5rem;
}
input {
    width: 100%;
    padding: 0.5rem;
    border: 1px solid #20B2AA;
}
@media (min-width: 600px) { /* Chapter 52 */
    .form-body {
        display: flex; /* Chapter 47 */
        gap: 1rem;
    }
    label, input {
        flex: 1;
    }
}
```

Test—<form-header> fades, <form-body> shadows on hover, flexes wide—styled <div>s!

Why Styling <div> Matters

- **Define**: <gallery> (Chapter 32) borders—e.g., sections pop.

- **Enhance**: <form> (Chapter 22) backgrounds—e.g., gradient depth.

- **Interact**: <video> (Chapter 26) hovers—e.g., motion cues.

- **Polish**: <h1> (Chapter 12) containers—e.g., standout intros.

Hands-On Practice

In "style.css":

- .wrapper { width: 90%; margin: 0 auto; padding: 1rem; background-color: #E0FFFF; border: 2px solid #4682B4; }.

- .top { padding: 15px; background-color: #FF4500; color: white; text-align: center; transition: transform 0.3s ease; }, .top:hover { transform: translateY(-5px); }.

- .content { padding: 20px; border: 1px dashed #32CD32; background-color: #FFF0F5; box-shadow: 0 2px 4px rgba(0, 0, 0, 0.1); }.

Add to "index.html":

```
<main>
    <div class="wrapper">
        <div class="top"><h1>Style Test</h1></div>
        <div class="content"><p>Styled div!</p></div>
    </div>
</main>
```

Test—resize, hover, check mobile. Does <top> lift? <content> shadow? Add comments—<!-- Styled divs -->. Play: add border-radius: 10px;, background-image—polish it!

Tips

- **Shadow**: box-shadow—soft edges.

- **Radius**: border-radius: 5px—rounded.

- **Test**: Hover—see motion.

What's Next

Styled <div>s shine—<span> (Chapter 60) tweaks inline for your <gallery>, <form>, and more!

Chapter 60
Using <span> for Inline Styling

<div>s group and style blocks (Chapters 58-59)—but what about tweaking *inside* lines? The <span> element is HTML5's inline stylist, wrapping bits of text or elements within <p>, <h1>, or <li> for pinpoint CSS flair. Think highlighting words, coloring phrases, or animating links—by the end, you'll use <span> to spice up your forms, galleries, and videos with inline magic. Let's span the details!

What's <span>?

- **Inline**: Sits in flow—unlike block <div> (Chapter 57).

- **Neutral**: No meaning—pure styling, like <div> but slim.

- **CSS**: Targets with classes—e.g., color, font-size.

Basic Use

```
<p>This is <span class="highlight">awesome</span>!</p>
```

CSS:

```
.highlight {
    color: #FF4500; /* Chapter 40 */
    font-weight: bold; /* Chapter 37 */
}
```

Test—awesome glows orange, bold—inline pop!

Inline vs. Block

```
<p>Normal <span class="special">special</span> text.</p>
```

```
<div class="block">Block text.</div>
```

CSS:

```
.special {
    background-color: #FFF0F5; /* Chapter 41 */
    padding: 2px 5px;
}
.block {
    background-color: #E0FFFF;
    padding: 10px;
}
```

<span> stays in line, <div> breaks—<span>'s subtle!

Practical Example

For your form (Chapter 22):

```
<main>
    <h1>Contact <span class="accent">Me</span></h1>
    <form>
        <p><label for="name">Name: <span class="required">*</
span></label></p>
        <input type="text" id="name" name="name">
    </form>
</main>
```

CSS:

```
* {
    box-sizing: border-box; /* Chapter 44 */
}
main {
    width: 90%;
```

```css
    margin: 0 auto; /* Chapter 45 */
    padding: 1rem; /* Chapter 53 */
    background-color: #F0FFF0;
}
h1 {
    font-size: 2rem;
    text-align: center;
    color: #8A2BE2;
}
.accent {
    color: #FF69B4;
    font-style: italic; /* Chapter 37 */
    transition: transform 0.3s ease; /* Chapter 54 */
}
.accent:hover {
    transform: scale(1.2); /* Chapter 55 */
}
.required {
    color: #FF4500;
    font-size: 1.2rem;
    animation: pulse 1s infinite; /* Chapter 56 */
}
@keyframes pulse {
    0% { transform: scale(1); }
    50% { transform: scale(1.3); }
    100% { transform: scale(1); }
}
label {
    display: block;
    margin-bottom: 0.5rem;
}
@media (min-width: 600px) { /* Chapter 52 */
    form {
        display: flex; /* Chapter 47 */
        gap: 1rem;
```

```
            }
    }
```

Test—<accent> pops pink, <required> pulses red—inline flair!

Why <span> Matters

- **Detail**: <p> phrases—e.g., <gallery> (Chapter 32) captions.

- **Cue**: <form> (Chapter 22) hints—e.g., required fields.

- **Motion**: <a> (Chapter 15) hovers—e.g., <video> (Chapter 26) links.

- **Subtle**: Inline tweaks—no layout shift.

Hands-On Practice

In "style.css":

- .highlight { color: #4682B4; background-color: #E0FFFF; padding: 2px 5px; font-weight: bold; }.

- .spin { display: inline-block; transition: transform 0.5s ease; }, .spin:hover { transform: rotate(360deg); }.

Add to "index.html":

```
<main>
    <p>This is <span class="highlight">really</span> cool!</p>
    <p>Check <span class="spin">this</span> out.</p>
</main>
```

Test—<highlight> stands out, <spin> twirls on hover. Add comments—<!-- Span styles -->. Play: add font-size: 1.2em;, background-image: linear-gradient—tweak inline!

Tips

- **Inline-Block**: display: inline-block;—for transforms.

- **Scope**: Small—<span> isn't <div>.

- **Test**: Hover—see effects.

Chapter 61
Creating Layouts with <div> and CSS

You've grouped and styled <div> elements (Chapters 58-59)—now let's use them to craft full layouts for your HTML5 site. Pairing <div> with CSS—Flexbox (Chapter 47), Grid (Chapter 48), and positioning—lets you build structured pages like a <header>-<main>-<footer> setup or a sidebar-content split. By the end, you'll arrange your <gallery>, <form>, and <video> into layouts that flow and flex, turning raw content into polished designs. Let's lay it out!

Why <div> for Layouts?

- **Blocks**: <div> stacks or aligns—perfect for sections.

- **Flexibility**: CSS molds—e.g., <gallery> (Chapter 32) rows.

- **Control**: Position—e.g., <form> (Chapter 22) sidebars.

- **Scale**: Responsive—e.g., <video> (Chapter 26) adjusts.

Basic Flex Layout

```
<div class="layout">

    <div class="header"><h1>My Site</h1></div>

    <div class="content"><p>Main content here.</p></div>

    <div class="footer"><p>© 2025</p></div>

</div>
```

CSS:

```
.layout {

    display: flex;

    flex-direction: column;

    width: 90%; /* Chapter 52 */
```

```css
        margin: 0 auto; /* Chapter 45 */
        gap: 1rem; /* Chapter 47 */
}
.header {
        background-color: #8A2BE2; /* Chapter 41 */
        color: white;
        padding: 1rem; /* Chapter 53 */
        text-align: center; /* Chapter 38 */
}
.content {
        padding: 1.5rem;
        background-color: #F0FFF0;
        border: 1px solid #4682B4; /* Chapter 43 */
}
.footer {
        background-color: #FF69B4;
        color: white;
        padding: 0.5rem;
        text-align: center;
}
```

Test it (Chapter 5)—stacked, clean layout—<div> powers structure!

Grid Layout Example

```html
<div class="grid-layout">
    <div class="header"><h1>My Site</h1></div>
    <div class="sidebar"><p>Links</p></div>
    <div class="main"><p>Content</p></div>
    <div class="footer"><p>© 2025</p></div>
</div>
```

CSS:

```
.grid-layout {
    display: grid; /* Chapter 48 */
    grid-template-areas:
        "header header"
        "sidebar main"
        "footer footer";
    grid-template-rows: 80px 1fr 60px;
    grid-template-columns: 200px 1fr;
    gap: 15px;
    width: 95%;
    margin: 0 auto;
}
.header { grid-area: header; background-color: #8A2BE2; color:
white; padding: 1rem; }
.sidebar { grid-area: sidebar; background-color: #E0FFFF; pad-
ding: 1rem; }
.main { grid-area: main; background-color: #F0FFF0; padding:
1rem; }
.footer { grid-area: footer; background-color: #FF69B4; color:
white; padding: 0.5rem; }
```

Test—2D layout—<header> spans, <sidebar> and <main> side-by-side—
<div> grids!

Practical Example

For your gallery (Chapter 32):

```
<div class="page-layout">
    <div class="header">
        <h1>My Photos</h1>
        <p>A collection</p>
    </div>
    <div class="gallery">
```

```
                <div class="gallery-inner">

                    <figure>

                        <img src="images/pic1.jpg" alt="Pic 1"
width="200">

                        <figcaption>One</figcaption>

                    </figure>

                    <figure>

                        <img src="images/pic2.jpg" alt="Pic 2"
width="200">

                        <figcaption>Two</figcaption>

                    </figure>

                </div>

            </div>

            <div class="footer">

                <p>© 2025</p>

            </div>

        </div>
```

CSS:

```
* {

    box-sizing: border-box; /* Chapter 44 */

}

.page-layout {

    display: flex;

    flex-direction: column;

    width: 90%;

    margin: 0 auto;

    gap: 1.5rem;

    background-color: #F0FFF0;

    padding: 1rem;

}

.header {

    background-image: linear-gradient(to right, #8A2BE2,
```

```css
#FF69B4); /* Chapter 42 */
    color: white;
    padding: 20px;
    text-align: center;
    border-bottom: 2px solid #FF4500;
}
h1 {
    font-size: 2rem; /* Chapter 53 */
    margin: 0 0 10px;
}
.gallery {
    padding: 15px;
    border: 1px solid #20B2AA;
    background-color: #FFF0F5;
}
.gallery-inner {
    display: grid; /* Chapter 48 */
    grid-template-columns: repeat(auto-fit, minmax(200px, 1fr));
    gap: 1rem;
    transition: transform 0.3s ease; /* Chapter 54 */
}
.gallery-inner:hover {
    transform: scale(1.02); /* Chapter 55 */
}
.footer {
    background-color: #4682B4;
    color: white;
    padding: 10px;
    text-align: center;
}
@media (min-width: 600px) { /* Chapter 52 */
    .page-layout {
        width: 80%;
```

```
        }
    }
```

Test—<header> intros, <gallery> grids inside <div>, <footer> closes—layout perfection!

Why Layouts with <div> Matter

- **Flow**: <form> (Chapter 22) splits—e.g., header + body.

- **Order**: <gallery> (Chapter 32) organizes—e.g., nested grids.

- **Polish**: <video> (Chapter 26) frames—e.g., header-content.

- **Scale**: Responsive—<div> adapts.

Hands-On Practice

In "style.css":

- .layout { display: grid; grid-template-areas: "top top" "side main" "bottom bottom"; grid-template-rows: 100px 1fr 50px; grid-template-columns: 200px 1fr; gap: 20px; width: 90%; margin: 0 auto; background-color: #E0FFFF; }.

- .top { grid-area: top; background-color: #FF4500; color: white; padding: 15px; }.

- .side { grid-area: side; padding: 10px; border: 1px solid #32CD32; }.

- .main { grid-area: main; padding: 15px; background-color: #FFF0F5; }.

Add to "index.html":

```
<div class="layout">
    <div class="top"><h1>Layout Test</h1></div>
    <div class="side"><p>Sidebar</p></div>
    <div class="main"><p>Main content</p></div>
    <div class="footer"><p>Footer</p></div>
</div>
```

Test—resize, zoom, check mobile. Does it grid? Add comments (Chapter 10)—<!-- Div layout -->. Play: switch to flex, adjust columns—shape it!

Tips

- **Nest**: <div> in <div>—deep layouts.

- **Debug**: border—see boxes.

- **Flex/Grid**: Mix—e.g., <gallery-inner> grids.

What's Next

Layouts with <div> structure—pop-ups (Chapter 62) add interactivity to your <gallery>, <form>, and more!

Chapter 62

Creating a Simple Pop-Up
with HTML and CSS

Your <div> layouts are solid (Chapter 61)—now let's add interactivity with a pop-up. Using HTML <div> and CSS display, you'll create a simple modal—a box that appears over content—for your HTML5 site's galleries, forms, or videos. Think image previews or info alerts—by the end, you'll build a pop-up triggered by a <button>, setting the stage for styling and JS enhancements. Let's pop it up!

What's a Pop-Up?

A modal is an overlay—content atop your page, dimming the rest. Here, <div> and CSS toggle visibility—no JS yet (Chapter 65 teases it).

Basic Pop-Up

```
<button class="open-btn">Show Pop-Up</button>

<div class="modal">

    <p>This is a pop-up!</p>

</div>
```

CSS:

```
.modal {

    display: none; /* Hidden */

    position: fixed; /* Overlays */

    top: 50%;

    left: 50%;

    transform: translate(-50%, -50%); /* Center */

    background-color: #FFF;

    padding: 20px;
```

```
    border: 1px solid #4682B4; /* Chapter 43 */
}
.open-btn {
    padding: 10px;
    background-color: #FF69B4;
    color: white;
    border: none;
}
```

Test—<modal> hides—needs JS (later) or manual CSS toggle for now.

Toggle with CSS (Hack)

```
<input type="checkbox" id="toggle" class="toggle">
<label for="toggle" class="open-btn">Show Pop-Up</label>
<div class="modal">
    <p>Pop-up content!</p>
</div>
```

CSS:

```
.toggle {
    display: none;
}
.modal {
    display: none;
    position: fixed;
    top: 50%;
    left: 50%;
    transform: translate(-50%, -50%);
    background-color: #FFF0F5;
    padding: 20px;
    border: 1px solid #20B2AA;
}
```

```
.toggle:checked ~ .modal {
    display: block; /* Shows when checked */
}
.open-btn {
    padding: 10px 20px;
    background-color: #8A2BE2;
    color: white;
    cursor: pointer;
}
```

Test—click <label>, <modal> appears—checkbox hack works!

Practical Example

For your gallery (Chapter 32):

```
<main>
    <h1>My Photos</h1>
    <div class="gallery">
        <input type="checkbox" id="popup" class="toggle">
        <label for="popup" class="open-btn">View Info</label>
        <div class="modal">
            <h2>Gallery Details</h2>
            <p>This is my photo collection!</p>
        </div>
        <figure>
            <img src="images/pic1.jpg" alt="Pic 1" width="200">
            <figcaption>One</figcaption>
        </figure>
    </div>
</main>
```

CSS:

```css
* {
    box-sizing: border-box; /* Chapter 44 */
}
main {
    width: 90%;
    margin: 0 auto; /* Chapter 45 */
    padding: 1rem; /* Chapter 53 */
    background-color: #F0FFF0;
}
h1 {
    font-size: 2rem;
    text-align: center; /* Chapter 38 */
    color: #8A2BE2; /* Chapter 40 */
}
.gallery {
    display: flex; /* Chapter 47 */
    flex-wrap: wrap;
    gap: 1rem;
    padding: 15px;
    border: 1px solid #FF4500;
    position: relative; /* For modal */
}
.toggle {
    display: none;
}
.open-btn {
    padding: 10px 20px;
    background-color: #FF69B4;
    color: white;
    cursor: pointer;
    border: none;
```

```css
        transition: transform 0.3s ease; /* Chapter 54 */
}
.open-btn:hover {
    transform: scale(1.1); /* Chapter 55 */
}
.modal {
    display: none;
    position: fixed;
    top: 50%;
    left: 50%;
    transform: translate(-50%, -50%);
    background-color: #FFF0F5;
    padding: 20px;
    border: 1px solid #20B2AA;
    animation: fadeIn 0.5s ease-in; /* Chapter 56 */
}
.toggle:checked ~ .modal {
    display: block;
}
@keyframes fadeIn {
    0% { opacity: 0; }
    100% { opacity: 1; }
}
@media (min-width: 600px) { /* Chapter 52 */
    .gallery {
        justify-content: space-around;
    }
}
```

Test—click button, <modal> fades in—gallery info pops!

Why Pop-Ups Matter

- **Info**: <gallery> (Chapter 32) details—e.g., image notes.

- **Action**: <form> (Chapter 22) confirm—e.g., submit alert.

- **Engage**: <video> (Chapter 26) overlay—e.g., play tips.

- **Prep**: Styling (Chapter 63) enhances.

Hands-On Practice

In "style.css":

- .trigger { padding: 10px; background-color: #4682B4; color: white; cursor: pointer; }.

- .popup { display: none; position: fixed; top: 50%; left: 50%; transform: translate(-50%, -50%); padding: 15px; background-color: #E0FFFF; border: 1px solid #32CD32; }.

- #toggle:checked ~ .popup { display: block; }.

Add to "index.html":

```
<main>
    <input type="checkbox" id="toggle" class="toggle">
    <label for="toggle" class="trigger">Open</label>
    <div class="popup"><p>Pop-up!</p></div>
</main>
```

Test—click, <popup> shows. Add comments—<!-- Simple pop-up -->. Play: add transform: scale(0) at 0% in @keyframes—grow it!

Tips

- **Position**: fixed—overlays all.

- **Hack**: Checkbox—JS-free toggle.

- **Test**: Click—ensure visibility.

What's Next

Simple pop-ups appear—styling modals (Chapter 63) refines your <gallery>, <form>, and more!

Chapter 63
Styling Modals

Your pop-up works (Chapter 62)—now let's make it gorgeous with CSS. Styling modals involves tweaking <div>'s background, border, padding, and adding shadows or animations to enhance your HTML5 site's galleries, forms, or videos. By the end, you'll polish your modal into a sleek overlay, ready for <img> previews or <form> messages—professional and eye-catching. Let's style that pop!

Why Style Modals?

* **Appeal**: <gallery> (Chapter 32) preview—e.g., elegant image pop.

* **Clarity**: <form> (Chapter 22) alert—e.g., clear submit box.

* **Depth**: <video> (Chapter 26) overlay—e.g., styled controls.

* **Usability**: Visual cues—e.g., shadow focus.

Basic Styling

```css
.modal {
    display: none;
    position: fixed;
    top: 50%;
    left: 50%;
    transform: translate(-50%, -50%); /* Chapter 45 */
    background-color: #FFF;
    padding: 20px;
    border: 1px solid #4682B4;
    box-shadow: 0 4px 8px rgba(0, 0, 0, 0.2); /* Shadow */
    border-radius: 10px; /* Rounded */
}
```

Test with <div class="modal"><p>Styled!</p></div>—shadowed, rounded—pro look!

Enhanced Styling

```
.modal {
    display: none;
    position: fixed;
    top: 50%;
    left: 50%;
    transform: translate(-50%, -50%);
    background-image: linear-gradient(to bottom, #FFF0F5,
#E0FFFF); /* Chapter 42 */
    padding: 25px;
    border: 2px solid #FF69B4;
    border-radius: 15px;
    box-shadow: 0 6px 12px rgba(0, 0, 0, 0.3);
    width: 300px;
    max-width: 90%; /* Chapter 52 */
    transition: transform 0.3s ease, opacity 0.3s ease; /* Chap-
ter 54 */
}
.toggle:checked ~ .modal {
    display: block;
    transform: translate(-50%, -50%) scale(1.05); /* Chapter 55
*/
    opacity: 1;
}
```

Test—gradient, shadow, zoom—modal pops!

Practical Example

For your gallery (Chapter 32):

```
<main>
    <h1>My Photos</h1>
```

```
    <div class="gallery">
        <input type="checkbox" id="popup" class="toggle">
        <label for="popup" class="open-btn">View Info</label>
        <div class="modal">
            <h2>Photo Details</h2>
            <p>Shot in 2025!</p>
        </div>
        <figure>
            <img src="images/pic1.jpg" alt="Pic 1" width="200">
            <figcaption>One</figcaption>
        </figure>
    </div>
</main>
```

CSS:

```
* {
    box-sizing: border-box; /* Chapter 44 */
}
main {
    width: 90%;
    margin: 0 auto;
    padding: 1rem;
    background-color: #F0FFF0;
}
h1 {
    font-size: 2rem;
    text-align: center;
    color: #8A2BE2;
}
.gallery {
    display: flex;
    flex-wrap: wrap;
```

```css
    gap: 1rem;
    padding: 15px;
    border: 1px solid #FF4500;
    position: relative;
}
.toggle {
    display: none;
}
.open-btn {
    padding: 10px 20px;
    background-color: #FF69B4;
    color: white;
    border: none;
    border-radius: 5px;
    cursor: pointer;
    transition: background-color 0.3s ease;
}
.open-btn:hover {
    background-color: #FF1493;
}
.modal {
    display: none;
    position: fixed;
    top: 50%;
    left: 50%;
    transform: translate(-50%, -50%);
    background-color: #FFF0F5;
    padding: 20px;
    border: 2px solid #20B2AA;
    border-radius: 10px;
    box-shadow: 0 4px 8px rgba(0, 0, 0, 0.2);
    width: 300px;
    max-width: 90%;
```

```
    animation: slideIn 0.5s ease-in; /* Chapter 56 */
}
.toggle:checked ~ .modal {
    display: block;
}
@keyframes slideIn {
    0% { transform: translate(-50%, -60%); opacity: 0; }
    100% { transform: translate(-50%, -50%); opacity: 1; }
}
h2 {
    margin: 0 0 10px;
    color: #4682B4;
}
@media (min-width: 600px) {
    .gallery {
        justify-content: space-around;
    }
}
```

Test—click, <modal> slides in, styled—gallery info shines!

Why Styling Modals Matters

- **Pro**: <gallery> (Chapter 32) previews—e.g., sleek pop.

- **Clear**: <form> (Chapter 22) messages—e.g., styled alert.

- **Depth**: <video> (Chapter 26) overlays—e.g., shadow lift.

- **Engage**: Animations—e.g., <button> (Chapter 25) cues.

Hands-On Practice

In "style.css":

- .trigger { padding: 10px; background-color: #4682B4; color: white; border-radius: 5px; cursor: pointer; }.

- .popup { display: none; position: fixed; top: 50%; left: 50%; transform: translate(-50%, -50%); width: 250px; padding: 15px; background-color: #E0FFFF; border: 1px solid #32CD32; border-radius: 8px; box-shadow: 0 2px 6px rgba(0, 0, 0, 0.1); transition: transform 0.3s ease; }, #toggle:checked ~ .popup { display: block; transform: translate(-50%, -50%) scale(1.1); }.

Add to "index.html":

```
<main>
    <input type="checkbox" id="toggle" class="toggle">
    <label for="toggle" class="trigger">Open</label>
    <div class="popup"><p>Styled pop-up!</p></div>
</main>
```

Test—click, <popup> grows, shadows. Add comments—<!-- Styled modal -->. Play: add background-image, animation—fancy it!

Tips

- **Max**: max-width—fits screens.

- **Shadow**: box-shadow—lifts off page.

- **Test**: Resize—centers well?

Chapter 64
Adding Close Buttons and Overlays

You've styled sleek modals (Chapter 63)—now let's make them practical with close buttons and overlays. A close button lets users dismiss your pop-up, while an overlay dims the background, focusing attention on your HTML5 site's <gallery> previews, <form> messages, or <video> info. By the end, you'll enhance your modals with a <button> to close and a <div> overlay, turning simple pop-ups into user-friendly features. Let's button it up and layer it on!

Why Close Buttons and Overlays?

- **Usability**: <button> closes—e.g., <gallery> (Chapter 32) preview done.

- **Focus**: Overlay dims—e.g., <form> (Chapter 22) alert stands out.

- **Pro**: <video> (Chapter 26) overlay—e.g., polished UI.

- **Control**: Users exit—e.g., no stuck modals.

Basic Setup with Close Button

```
<input type="checkbox" id="toggle" class="toggle">
<label for="toggle" class="open-btn">Open</label>
<div class="modal">
    <p>Pop-up content!</p>
    <button class="close-btn">Close</button>
</div>
```

CSS:

```
.toggle {
    display: none;
```

```css
}
.open-btn {
    padding: 10px 20px;
    background-color: #FF69B4;
    color: white;
    border: none;
    cursor: pointer;
}
.modal {
    display: none;
    position: fixed;
    top: 50%;
    left: 50%;
    transform: translate(-50%, -50%);
    background-color: #FFF0F5;
    padding: 20px;
    border: 1px solid #20B2AA;
    border-radius: 10px; /* Chapter 63 */
}
.toggle:checked ~ .modal {
    display: block;
}
.close-btn {
    padding: 5px 10px;
    background-color: #FF4500;
    color: white;
    border: none;
    border-radius: 5px;
    cursor: pointer;
    transition: background-color 0.3s ease; /* Chapter 54 */
}
.close-btn:hover {
    background-color: #CC3700;
}
```

Test (Chapter 5)—click <open-btn>, <modal> shows; <close-btn> needs JS (next chapter) or CSS hack to close for now.

Adding an Overlay

```html
<input type="checkbox" id="toggle" class="toggle">
<label for="toggle" class="open-btn">Open</label>
<div class="overlay"></div>
<div class="modal">
    <p>Pop-up with overlay!</p>
    <button class="close-btn">Close</button>
</div>
```

CSS:

```css
.overlay {
    display: none;
    position: fixed;
    top: 0;
    left: 0;
    width: 100%;
    height: 100%;
    background-color: rgba(0, 0, 0, 0.5); /* Semi-transparent black */
}
.toggle:checked ~ .overlay {
    display: block;
}
.modal {
    z-index: 10; /* Above overlay */
}
.toggle:checked ~ .modal {
    display: block;
}
```

Test—click, <overlay> dims, <modal> pops—focus achieved!

Practical Example

For your gallery (Chapter 32):

```html
<main>
    <h1>My Photos</h1>
    <div class="gallery">
        <input type="checkbox" id="popup" class="toggle">
        <label for="popup" class="open-btn">View Info</label>
        <div class="overlay"></div>
        <div class="modal">
            <h2>Photo Details</h2>
            <p>Shot in 2025!</p>
            <label for="popup" class="close-btn">Close</label>
        </div>
        <figure>
            <img src="images/pic1.jpg" alt="Pic 1" width="200">
            <figcaption>One</figcaption>
        </figure>
    </div>
</main>
```

CSS:

```css
* {
    box-sizing: border-box; /* Chapter 44 */
}
main {
    width: 90%;
    margin: 0 auto; /* Chapter 45 */
    padding: 1rem; /* Chapter 53 */
    background-color: #F0FFF0;
}
```

```css
h1 {
    font-size: 2rem;
    text-align: center; /* Chapter 38 */
    color: #8A2BE2; /* Chapter 40 */
}
.gallery {
    display: flex; /* Chapter 47 */
    flex-wrap: wrap;
    gap: 1rem;
    padding: 15px;
    border: 1px solid #FF4500;
    position: relative;
}
.toggle {
    display: none;
}
.open-btn {
    padding: 10px 20px;
    background-color: #FF69B4;
    color: white;
    border: none;
    border-radius: 5px;
    cursor: pointer;
    transition: transform 0.3s ease; /* Chapter 54 */
}
.open-btn:hover {
    transform: scale(1.1); /* Chapter 55 */
}
.overlay {
    display: none;
    position: fixed;
    top: 0;
    left: 0;
```

```css
    width: 100%;
    height: 100%;
    background-color: rgba(0, 0, 0, 0.6);
}
.modal {
    display: none;
    position: fixed;
    top: 50%;
    left: 50%;
    transform: translate(-50%, -50%);
    background-color: #FFF0F5;
    padding: 20px;
    border: 2px solid #20B2AA;
    border-radius: 10px;
    box-shadow: 0 4px 8px rgba(0, 0, 0, 0.2); /* Chapter 63 */
    z-index: 10;
    animation: slideIn 0.5s ease-in; /* Chapter 56 */
}
.toggle:checked ~ .overlay,
.toggle:checked ~ .modal {
    display: block;
}
.close-btn {
    display: block;
    margin-top: 10px;
    padding: 8px 16px;
    background-color: #FF4500;
    color: white;
    border: none;
    border-radius: 5px;
    cursor: pointer;
    text-align: center;
}
```

```
.close-btn:hover {

    background-color: #CC3700;

}

@keyframes slideIn {

    0% { transform: translate(-50%, -60%); opacity: 0; }

    100% { transform: translate(-50%, -50%); opacity: 1; }

}

@media (min-width: 600px) { /* Chapter 52 */

    .gallery {

        justify-content: space-around;

    }

}
```

Test—click <open-btn>, <overlay> dims, <modal> slides in; click <close-btn> (as <label>), it hides—functional modal!

Why They Matter

- **Exit**: <close-btn>—e.g., <gallery> (Chapter 32) preview closes.

- **Focus**: <overlay>—e.g., <form> (Chapter 22) submit pops.

- **Depth**: <video> (Chapter 26)—e.g., overlay dims page.

- **Prep**: JS (Chapter 65)—e.g., dynamic toggle.

Hands-On Practice

In "style.css":

- .trigger { padding: 10px; background-color: #4682B4; color: white; border-radius: 5px; cursor: pointer; }.

- .overlay { display: none; position: fixed; top: 0; left: 0; width: 100%; height: 100%; background-color: rgba(0, 0, 0, 0.5); }.

- .popup { display: none; position: fixed; top: 50%; left: 50%; transform: translate(-50%, -50%); width: 250px; padding: 15px; background-color: #E0FFFF; border: 1px solid #32CD32; border-radius: 8px; box-shadow: 0 2px 6px rgba(0, 0, 0, 0.1); }.

- #toggle:checked ~ .overlay, #toggle:checked ~ .popup { display: block; }.

- .close { padding: 5px 10px; background-color: #FF4500; color: white; border: none; cursor: pointer; }.

Add to "index.html":

```
<main>
    <input type="checkbox" id="toggle" class="toggle">
    <label for="toggle" class="trigger">Open</label>
    <div class="overlay"></div>
    <div class="popup">
        <p>Modal with overlay!</p>
        <label for="toggle" class="close">Close</label>
    </div>
</main>
```

Test—click, overlay dims, <popup> shows; click <close>, it hides. Add comments (Chapter 10)—<!-- Modal with overlay -->. Play: tweak rgba, add animation—enhance it!

Tips

- **Z-Index**: <modal> above <overlay>—e.g., z-index: 10.

- **Opacity**: rgba—adjust dimness.

- **Test**: Click—ensure toggle.

What's Next

Buttons and overlays work—JS (Chapter 65) adds interactivity to your <gallery>, <form>, and more!

Chapter 65

Using JavaScript for Interactive Pop-Ups (Optional)

Your modals close with CSS hacks (Chapter 64)—now let's make them truly interactive with JavaScript (JS). JS toggles your HTML5 pop-ups dynamically—no checkbox tricks—enhancing <gallery> previews, <form> alerts, or <video> overlays. This optional chapter introduces basic JS, linking <button> clicks to show/hide <div> modals. By the end, you'll add scripted flair, making your site more engaging. Let's script it up!

Why JS for Pop-Ups?

- **Dynamic**: <button> toggles—e.g., <gallery> (Chapter 32) preview.

- **Control**: No hacks—e.g., <form> (Chapter 22) submit pop.

- **Future**: <video> (Chapter 26) play—e.g., scripted UI.

- **Power**: Beyond CSS—e.g., logic, events.

Basic JS Toggle

```
<button class="open-btn">Open</button>
<div class="modal">
    <p>Interactive pop-up!</p>
    <button class="close-btn">Close</button>
</div>
<script>
    const openBtn = document.querySelector('.open-btn');
    const modal = document.querySelector('.modal');
    const closeBtn = document.querySelector('.close-btn');

    openBtn.addEventListener('click', () => {
```

```
                    modal.style.display = 'block';
        });
        closeBtn.addEventListener('click', () => {
                    modal.style.display = 'none';
        });
</script>
```

CSS:

```css
.modal {
    display: none;
    position: fixed;
    top: 50%;
    left: 50%;
    transform: translate(-50%, -50%);
    background-color: #FFF0F5;
    padding: 20px;
    border: 1px solid #20B2AA;
}
.open-btn, .close-btn {
    padding: 10px 20px;
    background-color: #FF69B4;
    color: white;
    border: none;
    cursor: pointer;
}
.close-btn {
    background-color: #FF4500;
}
```

Test—click <open-btn>, <modal> shows; <close-btn>, hides—JS power!

Adding Overlay

```html
<button class="open-btn">Open</button>
<div class="overlay"></div>
<div class="modal">
    <p>Pop-up with overlay!</p>
    <button class="close-btn">Close</button>
</div>
<script>
    const openBtn = document.querySelector('.open-btn');
    const modal = document.querySelector('.modal');
    const overlay = document.querySelector('.overlay');
    const closeBtn = document.querySelector('.close-btn');

    function openModal() {
        modal.style.display = 'block';
        overlay.style.display = 'block';
    }
    function closeModal() {
        modal.style.display = 'none';
        overlay.style.display = 'none';
    }

    openBtn.addEventListener('click', openModal);
    closeBtn.addEventListener('click', closeModal);
    overlay.addEventListener('click', closeModal); // Click overlay to close
</script>
```

CSS:

```
.overlay {
    display: none;
    position: fixed;
    top: 0;
    left: 0;
    width: 100%;
    height: 100%;
    background-color: rgba(0, 0, 0, 0.6);
}
.modal {
    z-index: 10;
    border-radius: 10px; /* Chapter 63 */
    box-shadow: 0 4px 8px rgba(0, 0, 0, 0.2);
}
```

Test—click opens, overlay dims, click <close-btn> or <overlay> shuts—smooth!

Practical Example

For your gallery (Chapter 32):

```
<main>
    <h1>My Photos</h1>
    <div class="gallery">
        <button class="open-btn">View Info</button>
        <div class="overlay"></div>
        <div class="modal">
            <h2>Photo Details</h2>
            <p>Shot in 2025!</p>
            <button class="close-btn">Close</button>
        </div>
        <figure>
```

```
                <img src="images/pic1.jpg" alt="Pic 1" width="200">
            <figcaption>One</figcaption>
        </figure>
    </div>
</main>
<script>
    const openBtn = document.querySelector('.open-btn');
    const modal = document.querySelector('.modal');
    const overlay = document.querySelector('.overlay');
    const closeBtn = document.querySelector('.close-btn');

    openBtn.addEventListener('click', () => {
        modal.style.display = 'block';
        overlay.style.display = 'block';
    });
    closeBtn.addEventListener('click', () => {
        modal.style.display = 'none';
        overlay.style.display = 'none';
    });
    overlay.addEventListener('click', () => {
        modal.style.display = 'none';
        overlay.style.display = 'none';
    });
</script>
```

CSS (from Chapter 63, adjusted):

```
.gallery {
    display: flex; /* Chapter 47 */
    flex-wrap: wrap;
    gap: 1rem;
    padding: 15px;
    border: 1px solid #FF4500;
```

```
}
.open-btn {
    transition: transform 0.3s ease; /* Chapter 54 */
}
.open-btn:hover {
    transform: scale(1.1); /* Chapter 55 */
}
.overlay {
    background-color: rgba(0, 0, 0, 0.6);
}
.modal {
    animation: slideIn 0.5s ease-in; /* Chapter 56 */
}
```

Test—click, modal and overlay show; click either to close—interactive <gallery>!

Why JS Matters

- **Smooth**: <gallery> (Chapter 32)—e.g., preview toggle.

- **Logic**: <form> (Chapter 22)—e.g., submit pop-up.

- **Flex**: <video> (Chapter 26)—e.g., dynamic UI.

- **Start**: JS intro—more to come!

Hands-On Practice

In "style.css" (same as above), add to "index.html":

```
<main>
    <button class="open-btn">Open</button>
    <div class="overlay"></div>
    <div class="popup">
        <p>JS Pop-up!</p>
        <button class="close-btn">Close</button>
    </div>
</main>
```

```
<script>
    const openBtn = document.querySelector('.open-btn');

    const popup = document.querySelector('.popup');

    const overlay = document.querySelector('.overlay');

    const closeBtn = document.querySelector('.close-btn');


    openBtn.addEventListener('click', () => {
        popup.style.display = 'block';
        overlay.style.display = 'block';
    });
    closeBtn.addEventListener('click', () => {
        popup.style.display = 'none';
        overlay.style.display = 'none';
    });
    overlay.addEventListener('click', () => {
        popup.style.display = 'none';
        overlay.style.display = 'none';
    });
</script>
```

Test—click, <popup> shows; close via button or overlay. Add comments—<!-- JS pop-up -->. Play: add console.log('Opened!'); in JS—see DevTools console!

Tips

- **Query**: .class—match CSS (Chapter 36).

- **Events**: click—simple start.

- **Test**: DevTools—check JS runs.

What's Next

JS toggles pop-ups—what's next (Chapter 66) wraps your <gallery>, <form>, and more!

Chapter 66
What's Next?

You've built a stellar HTML5 and CSS site—forms, galleries, videos, styled <div>s, and interactive pop-ups (Chapters 1-65). Now what? This chapter reflects on your journey and previews next steps—more JS, server-side fun, or polishing your skills—to take your <gallery>, <form>, and <video> pages further. By the end, you'll have a roadmap to keep growing as a web creator. Let's look ahead!

Where You Are

- **HTML5**: <form> (Chapter 22), <video> (Chapter 26), <gallery> (Chapter 32)—structured.

- **CSS**: Flexbox (Chapter 47), Grid (Chapter 48), animations (Chapter 56)—styled.

- **JS**: Pop-ups (Chapter 65)—interactive start.

Next Steps

1. **More JS**:

   o Events: <form> submit—e.g., validate inputs (Chapter 24).

   o DOM: Change <h1> text—e.g., <gallery> titles.

   o Fetch: Load <img>—e.g., dynamic <gallery>.

2. **Server-Side**:

   o <form> action—e.g., save data (PHP, Node.js).

   o <video> hosting—e.g., stream uploads.

   o Database—e.g., <gallery> storage.

3. **Polish**:

   o Accessibility: <form> labels (Chapter 23)—screen readers.

- o Performance: <img> compression (Chapter 21)—faster loads.

- o Design: <div> shadows (Chapter 59)—UI tweaks.

Simple JS Next Step

```
<main>
    <h1 id="title">My Site</h1>
    <button onclick="document.getElementById('title').textCon-
tent='Changed!'">Change</button>
</main>
```

Test—click, <h1> updates—JS taste!

Practical Example

For your gallery:

```
<main>
    <h1>My Photos</h1>
    <div class="gallery">
        <button class="open-btn">View Info</button>
        <div class="overlay"></div>
        <div class="modal">
            <h2 id="modal-title">Photo Details</h2>
            <p>Shot in 2025!</p>
            <button class="close-btn">Close</button>
        </div>
        <figure>
            <img src="images/pic1.jpg" alt="Pic 1" width="200">
            <figcaption>One</figcaption>
        </figure>
    </div>
</main>
<script>
    const openBtn = document.querySelector('.open-btn');
```

```
      const modal = document.querySelector('.modal');

      const overlay = document.querySelector('.overlay');

      const closeBtn = document.querySelector('.close-btn');

      const title = document.querySelector('#modal-title');


      openBtn.addEventListener('click', () => {

          modal.style.display = 'block';

          overlay.style.display = 'block';

          title.textContent = 'Gallery Info'; // Dynamic

      });

      closeBtn.addEventListener('click', () => {

          modal.style.display = 'none';

          overlay.style.display = 'none';

      });

      overlay.addEventListener('click', () => {

          modal.style.display = 'none';

          overlay.style.display = 'none';

      });

  </script>
```

Test—click, <modal-title> updates—JS next step!

Why Keep Going?

- **Skills**: <form> submits—e.g., real apps.

- **Users**: <gallery> grows—e.g., dynamic content.

- **Fun**: <video> plays—e.g., custom controls.

Hands-On Practice

Add to "index.html":

```
<main>

    <h1 id="title">Next Steps</h1>

    <button onclick="document.getElementById('title').style.col-
or='#FF4500'">Color</button>
```

```
        </main>
```

Test—click, <h1> turns orange—JS taste. Add comments—<!-- Next JS
-->. Play: change textContent, add <form> submit—explore!

Tips

- **Learn**: JS basics—w3schools, MDN.

- **Tools**: VS Code (Chapter 4)—JS linting.

- **Test**: Console—console.log().

Chapter 67
Ensuring Robust Web Experiences

Cross-Browser Compatibility

In an ideal world, every web browser would render HTML, CSS, and JavaScript identically, and developers could write code once and trust it to work everywhere. However, the reality is far messier. Browsers like Chrome, Firefox, Safari, Edge, and even older versions of Internet Explorer interpret web standards differently due to variations in rendering engines (e.g., Blink, Gecko, WebKit), historical quirks, and vendor-specific features. Cross-browser compatibility is the art of ensuring your website looks and functions consistently across this diverse landscape.

Why It Matters

Your users don't all use the same browser. Some prefer Chrome for its speed, others stick to Safari on their iPhones, and a few might still cling to outdated versions of Internet Explorer for legacy reasons. If your site breaks in one browser, you risk alienating a portion of your audience. Beyond user experience, search engines like Google may penalize sites that don't perform well across platforms, impacting your SEO.

Strategies for Cross-Browser Compatibility

1. **Know Your Audience**: Use analytics tools (e.g., Google Analytics) to identify which browsers your visitors use most. Focus your efforts on those, but don't ignore edge cases entirely.

2. **Use Feature Detection**: Instead of assuming a browser supports a feature, check for it with tools like Modernizr. For example:

```
if (Modernizr.flexbox) {

    // Use Flexbox

} else {

    // Fallback to floats or inline-block

}
```

3. **Normalize CSS**: Browsers apply default styles differently (e.g., margins, padding). A CSS reset or normalization library like Normalize.css ensures a consistent starting point.

4. **Vendor Prefixes**: Some CSS properties (e.g., transition, transform) require prefixes like -webkit-, -moz-, or -ms- for full support. Use a tool like Autoprefixer to automate this:

```
.box {

    -webkit-transition: all 0.3s ease;

    -moz-transition: all 0.3s ease;

    transition: all 0.3s ease;

}
```

5. **Progressive Enhancement**: Build a solid, functional base that works everywhere, then layer on advanced features for modern browsers. For instance, a form should submit without JavaScript, but you can enhance it with AJAX for supported browsers.

6. **Test Early and Often**: Use tools like BrowserStack, Sauce Labs, or virtual machines to test your site across browsers and devices. Don't wait until the end—test as you build.

Common Pitfalls

- **CSS Grid and Flexbox**: Widely supported now, but older browsers (e.g., IE11) need fallbacks.

- **JavaScript Features**: ES6+ features (e.g., arrow functions, let/const) break in older browsers unless transpiled with Babel.

- **Media Queries**: Safari sometimes interprets units like vh differently—test responsive designs thoroughly.

By prioritizing compatibility, you ensure your site is accessible to as many users as possible, enhancing both reach and reputation.

Validating HTML and CSS

Validation is like proofreading your code—it ensures your HTML and CSS adhere to web standards set by the World Wide Web Consortium (W3C). While browsers are forgiving and often render sloppy code, unvalidated markup can lead to unpredictable behavior, accessibility issues, and maintenance headaches.

Why Validate?

- **Consistency**: Valid code is more likely to render consistently across browsers.

- **Accessibility**: Screen readers and assistive technologies rely on proper HTML structure.

- **Debugging**: Validation catches errors (e.g., unclosed tags) that might otherwise go unnoticed.

- **Professionalism**: Clean, standards-compliant code signals quality to clients and peers.

Tools for Validation

1. **W3C Markup Validator**: Upload your HTML file or paste a URL into validator.w3.org to check for errors. It flags issues like missing closing tags or invalid attributes:

```
<div>
    <p>Hello world <!-- Missing </p> -->
</div>
```

Error: "End tag div seen, but there were open elements."

2. **W3C CSS Validator**: At jigsaw.w3.org/css-validator, you can validate your stylesheets. It catches syntax errors or unsupported properties:

```
.box {
    colour: blue; /* Typo: should be "color" */
}
```

Error: "Unknown property colour."

3. **Browser Dev Tools**: Modern browsers highlight HTML errors in the console (e.g., Chrome's "Elements" tab shows unclosed tags).

How to Validate

- **Step 1**: Run your code through the validators after major changes.

- **Step 2**: Fix errors one by one—start with structural issues (e.g., nesting) before tackling warnings.

- **Step 3**: Retest to ensure fixes didn't introduce new problems.

Common Validation Issues

- **Unclosed Tags**: <div> without </div> confuses parsers.

- **Incorrect Nesting**: <p><div>Text</div></p> is invalid—block elements can't nest inside paragraphs.

- **Deprecated Elements**: <font> or <center> should be replaced with CSS.

- **Vendor-Specific CSS**: -webkit-box-shadow might trigger warnings, but it's often necessary for compatibility.

Validation isn't about perfection—it's about catching mistakes early and ensuring your foundation is solid.

Debugging Common Issues

Even with careful planning, things go wrong. A button doesn't click, a layout collapses, or a script throws an error. Debugging is the process of identifying and fixing these issues, and mastering it saves time and frustration.

Common Issues and Fixes

1. **Broken Layouts**

   o **Symptom**: Elements overlap or don't align.

   o **Cause**: CSS issues like float without clearfix, or position: absolute misuse.

   o **Fix**: Use browser dev tools (right-click > Inspect) to check computed styles. Add:

```css
.clearfix::after {
    content: "";
    display: table;
    clear: both;
}
```

   Or switch to Flexbox/Grid for modern layouts.

2. **JavaScript Errors**

   o **Symptom**: Console shows "Uncaught TypeError: Cannot read property 'X' of undefined."

   o **Cause**: Trying to access a property on a null/undefined object.

   o **Fix**: Check variable initialization:

```javascript
let element = document.getElementById('myId');
if (element) {
    element.style.color = 'red';
}
```

Use console.log() to trace values.

3. **Images Not Loading**

   o **Symptom**: Blank space or broken icon.

   o **Cause**: Wrong file path or missing file.

   o **Fix**: Inspect the <img> element's src in dev tools. Ensure case sensitivity matches (e.g., image.jpg vs. Image.JPG).

4. **Forms Not Submitting**

   o **Symptom**: Clicking "Submit" does nothing.

   o **Cause**: Missing action attribute or JavaScript intercepting the event.

   o **Fix**: Check:

```
<form action="/submit" method="POST">
```

And ensure event.preventDefault() isn't blocking submission unintentionally.

Debugging Tools

- **Browser Dev Tools**: Chrome's "Inspect" offers a console for JavaScript errors, a network tab for resource failures, and a styles pane for CSS.

- **Console Logging**: Sprinkle console.log('Here') to track execution flow.

- **Linters**: Tools like ESLint (JavaScript) or Stylelint (CSS) catch syntax errors before runtime.

- **Breakpoints**: In dev tools, set breakpoints in JavaScript to pause and inspect variables.

Debugging Workflow

1. **Reproduce**: Trigger the issue consistently.

2. **Isolate**: Narrow it down (e.g., comment out CSS blocks or disable scripts).

3. **Investigate**: Use tools to pinpoint the cause.

4. **Fix**: Apply the smallest change that resolves it.

5. **Test**: Verify across browsers and devices.

Pro Tip: Stay Calm

Debugging can feel like chasing ghosts, but patience pays off. Start with the obvious—typos, paths, permissions—then dig deeper. Every error teaches you something new about how the web works.

Chapter 68
Launching Your Website

Choosing a Hosting Provider

Your website is ready—beautifully coded, validated, and debugged. Now, it needs a home on the internet. A hosting provider is the service that stores your site's files and makes them accessible to the world. Choosing the right one is critical: it affects your site's speed, reliability, security, and even your budget. With countless options—shared hosting, VPS, dedicated servers, cloud hosting—how do you decide?

Why It Matters

A slow or unreliable host can frustrate users and hurt your search engine rankings. Downtime means lost visitors, and poor support can leave you stranded during emergencies. The right provider aligns with your site's needs and your technical comfort level.

Types of Hosting

1. **Shared Hosting**:

   o You share a server with other websites. Cheap (e.g., $3–$10/month) and beginner-friendly, but performance can suffer if neighbors get busy.

   o Best for: Small personal sites or blogs (e.g., Bluehost, HostGator).

2. **Virtual Private Server (VPS)**:

   o A virtual slice of a server, offering more control and re-sources. Pricier ($20–$50/month) and requires some server knowledge.

   o Best for: Growing sites with moderate traffic (e.g., Site-Ground, DigitalOcean).

3. **Dedicated Hosting**:

- o An entire server for your site. Expensive ($80–$200+/month) and powerful, but you manage everything.

- o Best for: High-traffic or resource-heavy sites (e.g., Liquid Web).

4. **Cloud Hosting**:

- o Scalable hosting across multiple servers. Flexible pricing based on usage, with excellent uptime.

- o Best for: Dynamic sites needing scalability (e.g., AWS, Google Cloud, Cloudways).

Key Factors to Consider

- **Uptime Guarantee**: Look for 99.9% or higher—every minute of downtime counts.

- **Speed**: Check for SSD storage, CDN support (e.g., Cloudflare), and server locations near your audience.

- **Support**: 24/7 customer service via chat, email, or phone is a life-saver.

- **Scalability**: Can you upgrade easily as your site grows?

- **Security**: SSL certificates, backups, and malware scanning should be standard.

- **Cost**: Balance features with your budget, but beware of "too cheap" deals with hidden limits.

How to Choose

1. **Define Your Needs**: A blog needs less power than an e-commerce site.

2. **Research Reviews**: Sites like Trustpilot or Reddit reveal real user experiences.

3. **Test Support**: Contact pre-sales support with a question—response time hints at their service quality.

4. **Trial Periods**: Many offer 30-day money-back guarantees (e.g., A2 Hosting).

Example Decision

For a small pet breeder directory (like SearchByBreed), shared hosting from SiteGround ($6/month) offers a great start: fast SSDs, free SSL, and solid support. As traffic grows, you could scale to their VPS-like "Cloud Hosting" plans.

A good host is your site's foundation—pick wisely, and it'll support your ambitions without breaking the bank.

Uploading Files via FTP

With a hosting provider secured, it's time to move your website from your computer to the server. FTP (File Transfer Protocol) is the classic method for uploading files—simple, reliable, and widely supported. Think of it as a digital courier shuttling your HTML, CSS, JavaScript, and images to their new home.

Why Use FTP?

FTP lets you manage server files directly: upload new pages, update styles, or delete old assets. It's essential for getting your site live and maintaining it over time.

Tools You'll Need

- **FTP Client**: Software like FileZilla (free), Cyberduck, or Transmit (Mac) simplifies the process.

- **Credentials**: Your host provides:

    o   Hostname (e.g., ftp.yourdomain.com or an IP like 192.168.1.1).

    o   Username and password.

    o   Port (usually 21 for FTP, 22 for SFTP—secure FTP).

Step-by-Step Guide

1. **Install an FTP Client**: Download FileZilla from filezilla-project. org and install it.

2. **Gather Credentials**: Log into your hosting control panel (e.g., cPanel) and find your FTP details under "FTP Accounts."

3. **Connect to the Server**:

    o   Open FileZilla.

    o   Enter the hostname, username, password, and port in the top fields.

o Click "Quickconnect." You'll see a "Successful connection" message.

4. **Navigate Folders**:

   o Left side: Your local computer files.

   o Right side: The server (look for public_html or www—your site's root directory).

5. **Upload Files**:

   o Drag files (e.g., index.html, css/style.css) from the left to public_html on the right.

   o Watch the transfer queue at the bottom—it'll confirm when done.

6. **Verify**: Visit yourdomain.com in a browser to see your live site.

Common Issues

- **Permission Denied**: Ensure files have proper permissions (e.g., 644 for files, 755 for directories). Fix in FileZilla: right-click > "File Permissions."

- **Wrong Directory**: Uploading outside public_html hides your site—double-check the path.

- **Connection Refused**: Verify credentials and ensure your host allows FTP (some use SFTP instead).

Pro Tip: Use SFTP

If your host supports it, switch to SFTP (Secure FTP) for encrypted transfers. It's safer and often just a toggle in your FTP client (port 22).

Uploading via FTP bridges the gap between local development and global access—your site's now live for the world to see!

Domain Names and DNS

Your site's on the server, but how do users find it? A domain name (e.g., yoursite.com) is your site's address, and DNS (Domain Name System) is the internet's phonebook, translating that name into a server IP (e.g., 192.168.1.1). Setting this up ties your hosting to a memorable URL.

Why It Matters

A custom domain builds trust and brand identity—yoursite.com beats 192.168.1.1/yoursite. DNS ensures that name points to your server, making your site reachable.

Buying a Domain

1. **Choose a Registrar**: GoDaddy, Namecheap, or Google Domains are popular choices.

2. **Pick a Name**: Short, memorable, and relevant (e.g., yoursite.com).

   o   Check availability—.com is king, but .co or .pet work too.

3. **Register**: Pay $10–$15/year. Enable auto-renew to avoid losing it.

Understanding DNS

- **A Record**: Links your domain to your server's IP (e.g., 192.168.1.1).

- **CNAME**: Aliases subdomains (e.g., www.yoursite.com to yoursite.com).

- **MX Records**: Directs email (e.g., for info@yoursite.com).

- **Nameservers**: Tells the internet which DNS server (usually your host's) manages your domain.

Connecting Domain to Hosting

1. **Get Your Host's Nameservers**: In your hosting panel (e.g., SiteGround), find something like:

   o   ns1.siteground.net

   o   ns2.siteground.net

2. **Update at Registrar**:

   o   Log into Namecheap (or your registrar).

   o   Go to "Domain Management" > "Nameservers."

   o   Select "Custom DNS" and enter your host's nameservers.

   o   Save—propagation takes 1–48 hours.

3. **Set Up DNS Records** (if needed):

   o   In your host's DNS manager, add an A record:

```
Type: A

Host: @

Value: 192.168.1.1 (your server IP)

TTL: 14400
```

    o   Add a CNAME for www:

```
Type: CNAME

Host: www

Value: yoursite.com
```

Testing It Out

- Ping your domain (ping yoursite.com) to confirm it resolves to your IP.

- Visit it in a browser—if you see your site, success!

Common Pitfalls

- **Propagation Delay**: DNS changes aren't instant—be patient.

- **Typo in Records**: Double-check IPs and nameservers.

- **No SSL**: After DNS is set, enable HTTPS via your host (e.g., Let's Encrypt).

With your domain and DNS configured, your site's address is official—ready for visitors to explore.

Chapter 69
Basics of SEO for HTML5

SEO (Search Engine Optimization) for HTML5 involves leveraging the semantic structure and features of HTML5 to make your site more crawlable and understandable to search engines like Google. Here's how to get started:

1. **Use Semantic Tags**: HTML5 introduces tags like <header>, <footer>, <nav>, <article>, and <section>. These help search engines understand the structure and hierarchy of your content. For example:

```
<header>

    <h1>My Website</h1>

    <nav>

        <ul>

            <li><a href="#home">Home</a></li>

            <li><a href="#about">About</a></li>

        </ul>

    </nav>

</header>
```

This tells crawlers what's navigation versus main content.

2. **Meta Tags**: Include essential meta tags in the <head> section for better indexing:

```
<meta charset="UTF-8">

<meta name="description" content="A brief description of your page">

<meta name="keywords" content="SEO, HTML5, web optimization">
```

```
<meta name="viewport" content="width=device-width, ini-
tial-scale=1.0">
```

The viewport tag is crucial for mobile responsiveness, a big SEO factor.

3. **Title Tags**: Keep them unique, descriptive, and under 60 characters:

```
<title>SEO Basics for HTML5 | Your Site</title>
```

4. **Alt Text for Accessibility**: Use alt attributes on images (more on this below) to improve accessibility and keyword relevance.

Optimizing Images and Assets

Images and other assets can slow down your site if not optimized, hurting both SEO and user experience.

1. **Compress Images**: Use tools like TinyPNG or ImageOptim to reduce file size without losing quality. Aim for formats like WebP, which offers better compression than JPEG or PNG.

```
<img src="example.webp" alt="Descriptive keyword-rich text" load-
ing="lazy">
```

2. **Use Descriptive Alt Text**: This helps search engines understand the image and boosts accessibility:

```
<img src="seo-optimized-image.webp" alt="SEO guide infographic
for HTML5">
```

3. **Lazy Loading**: Add the loading="lazy" attribute to defer offscreen images, speeding up initial page load:

```
<img src="footer-image.webp" alt="Footer design" loading="lazy">
```

4. **Responsive Images**: Use the <picture> element or srcset to serve different image sizes based on device:

```
<picture>

    <source media="(max-width: 600px)" srcset="small-image.webp">

    <img src="large-image.webp" alt="Responsive image example">

</picture>
```

5. **Optimize Other Assets**: Minify JavaScript files and use modern formats like SVG for icons to reduce load times.

Minifying CSS and HTML

Minification removes unnecessary characters (whitespace, comments, etc.) from your code, reducing file sizes and improving load speed.

1. **Minify CSS**: Tools like CSSNano or UglifyCSS can shrink your stylesheets. Before:

```
body {

    margin: 0;

    padding: 10px;

}
```

After:

```
body{margin:0;padding:10px}
```

2. **Minify HTML**: Use tools like HTMLMinifier. Before:

```
<html>

    <head>

        <title>My Site</title>
```

```
        </head>

    <body>

        <p>Hello World</p>

    </body>

</html>
```

After:

```
<html><head><title>My Site</title></head><body><p>Hello World</
p></body></html>
```

3. **Automate It**: Integrate minification into your build process with tools like Gulp or Webpack.

Improving Website Speed

Site speed is a direct ranking factor for Google, and HTML5 offers ways to optimize it.

1. **Enable Compression**: Use Gzip or Brotli on your server to compress files before sending them to the browser. Add this to your .htaccess (Apache):

```
<IfModule mod_deflate.c>

    AddOutputFilterByType DEFLATE text/html text/css appli-
cation/javascript

</IfModule>
```

2. **Leverage Browser Caching**: Set expiration headers so returning visitors load cached assets:

```
<IfModule mod_expires.c>

    ExpiresActive On

    ExpiresByType image/webp "access plus 1 month"

    ExpiresByType text/css "access plus 1 week"
```

```
        </IfModule>
```

3. **Reduce HTTP Requests**: Combine CSS/JS files where possible and use CSS sprites or inline small images as Data URIs.

4. **Critical CSS**: Inline critical CSS (styles needed for above-the-fold content) in the <head> to render pages faster:

```
<style>body{font-family:Arial;margin:0}</style>
```

5. **Test Your Speed**: Use tools like Google PageSpeed Insights or GT-metrix to identify bottlenecks and get specific recommendations.

Putting It All Together

Here's a quick example of an optimized HTML5 snippet:

```
<!DOCTYPE html>
<html lang="en">
<head>
    <meta charset="UTF-8">
    <meta name="description" content="SEO-optimized HTML5 page">
    <meta name="viewport" content="width=device-width, ini-
tial-scale=1.0">
    <title>Fast SEO Page</title>
    <style>body{font-family:Arial;margin:0}</style>
    <link rel="stylesheet" href="styles.min.css">
</head>
<body>
    <header>
        <h1>Welcome</h1>
    </header>
    <main>
        <img src="optimized-image.webp" alt="SEO example" load-
ing="lazy">
```

```
    </main>

    <script src="scripts.min.js" defer></script>
</body>
</html>
```

This uses semantic tags, lazy loading, minified assets, and deferred scripts for optimal performance.

Chapter 70
Keeping Content Fresh

Congratulations! You've built an incredible HTML5 and CSS website from scratch, and it's live for the world to see. But here's the reality: a website isn't a one-and-done project. Just like a garden needs tending or a story needs new chapters, your site thrives when its content stays fresh. In this chapter, we'll explore why keeping your content updated matters and how to do it effectively—ensuring your site remains relevant, engaging, and valuable to your visitors.

Why Fresh Content Matters

Imagine visiting a blog with posts from 2015 or an online store with outdated product listings. It feels stale, doesn't it? Search engines like Google prioritize websites that regularly add new, high-quality content. This boosts your site's ranking, making it easier for people to find you when they search for terms like "men's clothing [your town]." Fresh content also keeps your audience coming back—whether they're reading your latest blog post or checking for new products in your WooCommerce store. A stagnant site risks losing trust and traffic, so let's keep it alive!

Strategies for Staying Current

1. **Regular Updates**
   Start with a schedule. If you run a blog, aim for a new post weekly or monthly—whatever you can manage. For a store, update product descriptions, add seasonal items, or run promotions. Use your HTML skills to create new pages (saved as .html files) or edit existing ones. For example, update your index.html with a banner announcing a sale.

2. **Leverage CSS for a Dynamic Look**
   Fresh content doesn't just mean new text—it's also about presentation. Tweak your CSS files (or the <style> tags in your HTML) to reflect changes. Add a seasonal color scheme—think warm oranges for fall—or animate a "New Arrival" section with a simple CSS transition. We covered these techniques earlier, so revisit those chapters to refresh your styling game.

3. **Engage Your Audience**
   Encourage interaction with calls-to-action. Add a comment section to your blog using HTML forms, or include a feedback link on your store page. Respond to visitors and incorporate their suggestions into new content. This keeps your site a living conversation, not a digital museum.

4. **Remove the Old**
   Outdated content can hurt more than help. If a blog post is irrelevant or a product is discontinued, archive it or delete it. Update your site's navigation (in your HTML) to reflect what's current, ensuring a seamless user experience across devices.

Tools to Simplify the Process

If you've integrated WordPress into your site (as we discussed earlier), use its dashboard to manage blog posts and store updates—it's a breeze compared to editing raw HTML files manually. For your custom PHP sections, write a simple script to automate minor updates, like rotating featured content. Keep your .css file organized with comments (e.g., /* Fall 2025 Styles */) to track changes easily.

A Practical Example

Let's say you run a site for a local bakery. Start with a baking-tips.html page sharing a recipe. Next month, add new-treats.html with photos of fresh pastries, styled with CSS to highlight them. Link both pages in your index.html, and update your styles.css with a warm color palette. Over time, archive old recipes and promote new ones—your site evolves with your business.

Making It a Habit

Set a reminder—weekly or monthly—to review your site. Check analytics (if you've added Google Analytics) to see what content works. If a page gets no visits, refresh it or replace it. Treat this like brushing your teeth: a small, consistent effort keeps things healthy.

By keeping your content fresh, you're not just maintaining a website—you're building a destination. Your visitors will notice the care, and search engines will reward the effort. So, grab your text editor, update that .html file, and let's keep your site thriving. The web waits for no one—let's make sure your corner of it stays vibrant!

Chapter 71
Backing Up Your Website

You've poured your heart into building a website from scratch—writing HTML5 files (saved as .html), styling them with CSS (either in <style> tags or .css files), and maybe even adding a WordPress blog or WooCommerce store. It's live, it's beautiful, and it's yours. But what happens if your server crashes, a plugin breaks your site, or—worst of all—you accidentally delete a crucial file? Without a backup, you could lose everything. In this chapter, we'll explore why backing up your website is non-negotiable and how to do it effectively, so your hard work stays safe.

Why Backups Are Essential

Websites are fragile. A hosting provider might experience downtime, a hacker might target your site, or a simple mistake—like overwriting index. html—can erase hours of work. Backups are your safety net. They let you restore your site to a working state, no matter what goes wrong. Think of it as insurance: you hope you'll never need it, but you'll be glad it's there when disaster strikes.

What to Back Up

Your website has two main parts to back up:

1. **Files**: This includes your .html files, .css files, images, and any PHP scripts.

How to Back Up Your Website

Let's break this into steps, covering both your custom HTML/CSS.

1. **Manual File Backups**
   Use an FTP client like Cyberduck to connect to your server. Download all your website files—your .html files, .css files and any media—to your computer. Save them in a folder labeled with the date, like website-backup-2025-03-17.

2. **Automate with Hosting Tools**
   Many hosting providers, like SiteGround or Hostinger, offer built-in backup services. Some are free, others are paid add-ons. Set up

daily or weekly backups to run automatically, and ensure you can access older versions (e.g., a backup from last month). This is a lifesaver for WordPress sites, where updates can sometimes break things.

3. **Store Backups Safely**
   Keep copies of your backups in multiple places: your computer, an external hard drive, and a cloud service (e.g., Google Drive, Dropbox). This protects you from hardware failures or lost devices.

Test Your Backups

A backup is only useful if it works. Once a month, try restoring a test version of your site using your backup files. For your HTML/CSS, open them in a browser to confirm they load correctly.

Make It a Habit

Set a calendar reminder to back up your site weekly—or daily if you update often. Treat it like watering a plant: a small effort now prevents a big headache later. With your backups in place, you can experiment with new CSS styles or HTML features fearlessly, knowing your work is secure.

Chapter 72

Coding... and Codes

Now that you read the book, you can see more codes and download for free full websites. This will help you build nice websites.

Check:

https://raphaelheide.com/book-html5

and type the code below to access:

H35AX

HTML5 Dictionary

<a>

Meaning: Creates a hyperlink to another page, file, or location (e.g., <a href="https://example.com">Link</a>).

<article>

Meaning: Defines a self-contained piece of content (e.g., a blog post) that can stand alone.

\<aside\>

Meaning: Marks content indirectly related to the main content, like side-bars or notes.

\<audio\>

Meaning: Embeds audio files, such as music or podcasts (e.g., \<audio src="song.mp3" controls\>\</audio\>).

\<b\>

Meaning: Boldens text for stylistic purposes without implying importance.

\<body\>

Meaning: Contains the visible content of an HTML document.

\<br\>

Meaning: Inserts a line break within text (self-closing tag).

\<canvas\>

Meaning: Provides a drawing area for graphics via JavaScript (e.g., animations or charts).

\<datalist\>

Meaning: Provides a predefined list of options for an \<input\> element (e.g., autocomplete suggestions).

\<div\>

Meaning: A block-level container for grouping content or applying styles.

\<figure\>

Meaning: Groups self-contained content like images or code, often with \<figcaption\>.

<footer>

Meaning: Represents the footer of a document or section (e.g., copyright info).

<form>

Meaning: Creates an interactive form for user input (e.g., <form action="/submit">).

<h1> to <h6>

Meaning: Defines headings, with <h1> being the highest level and <h6> the lowest.

<head>

Meaning: Contains metadata, scripts, and links (e.g., <title>, <meta>) not displayed on the page.

<header>

Meaning: Defines a header section, often with introductory content or navigation.

<html>

Meaning: The root element of an HTML document, enclosing all content.

<i>

Meaning: Italicizes text for stylistic purposes, often for emphasis or notation.

<img>

Meaning: Embeds an image (e.g., <img src="pic.jpg" alt="Description">).

<input>

Meaning: Creates an input field, with types like text, email, checkbox, etc.

<link>

Meaning: Links external resources, like CSS files (e.g., <link rel="stylesheet" href="styles.css">).

<meta>

Meaning: Provides metadata, such as character encoding (e.g., <meta charset="UTF-8">).

<nav>

Meaning: Defines a navigation section with links.

<p>

Meaning: Represents a paragraph of text.

<progress>

Meaning: Displays a progress bar (e.g., <progress value="50" max="100">).

<script>

Meaning: Embeds or links to JavaScript (e.g., <script src="script.js"></script>).

<section>

Meaning: Groups thematic content, typically with a heading.

<span>

Meaning: An inline container for styling or scripting small portions of content.

\<table>

Meaning: Creates a table, used with \<tr>, \<th>, and \<td> for rows, headers, and cells.

\<time>

Meaning: Represents a time or date (e.g., \<time datetime="2025-03-28">March 28, 2025\</time>).

\<ul>

Meaning: Creates an unordered (bulleted) list, used with \<li> for list items.

\<video>

Meaning: Embeds video content (e.g., \<video src="movie.mp4" controls>\</video>).

CSS3 Dictionary

align-items

Meaning: Aligns flex or grid items along the cross-axis (e.g., align-items: center;).

background-color

Meaning: Sets the background color (e.g., background-color: #ff0000; for red).

border

Meaning: Shorthand for border properties (e.g., border: 1px solid black;).

border-radius

Meaning: Rounds corners (e.g., border-radius: 5px;).

box-sizing

Meaning: Defines how width and height are calculated (e.g., box-sizing: border-box; includes padding and border).

color

Meaning: Sets text color (e.g., color: green;).

cursor

Meaning: Changes the mouse pointer style (e.g., cursor: pointer; for a hand icon).

display

Meaning: Controls element rendering (e.g., display: inline;, block, flex, or grid).

flex-direction

Meaning: Sets the direction of flex items (e.g., flex-direction: row; or column).

float

Meaning: Positions an element to the left or right, allowing content to wrap (e.g., float: left;).

font-size

Meaning: Sets text size (e.g., font-size: 16px;).

font-weight

Meaning: Adjusts text thickness (e.g., font-weight: bold; or 400).

gap

Meaning: Sets spacing between flex or grid items (e.g., gap: 10px;).

height

Meaning: Sets an element's height (e.g., height: 100px; or 50%).

justify-content

Meaning: Aligns flex or grid items along the main axis
(e.g., justify-content: space-between;).

margin

Meaning: Sets outside spacing (e.g., margin: 10px; or margin-top: 5px;).

max-width

Meaning: Limits an element's maximum width (e.g., max-width: 500px;).

opacity

Meaning: Adjusts transparency (e.g., opacity: 0.8; for 80% opaque).

overflow

Meaning: Controls content that exceeds an element's size
(e.g., overflow: scroll;).

padding

Meaning: Sets inside spacing (e.g., padding: 15px;).

position

Meaning: Sets positioning method
(e.g., position: relative;, absolute, or fixed).

text-align

Meaning: Aligns text horizontally (e.g., text-align: center;).

text-decoration

Meaning: Adds effects to text (e.g., text-decoration: underline; or none).

transition

Meaning: Animates property changes
(e.g., transition: background-color 0.5s;).

width

Meaning: Sets an element's width (e.g., width: 200px; or 100%).

z-index**

Meaning: Controls stacking order
(e.g., z-index: 100; places an element above others).

@keyframes

Meaning: Defines animation steps
(e.g., @keyframes fade { from { opacity: 0; } to { opacity: 1; } }).

@media

Meaning: Applies styles conditionally
(e.g., @media (min-width: 768px) { body { font-size: 18px; } }).